Women in Buddhist Tradition

Women in Buddhist Tradition

Sameer Das Gupta

CYBER TECH PUBLICATIONS
4264/3, Ansari Road, Daryaganj, New Delhi-110002 (India)
Ph.: 011-23244078. Fax: 011-23280028
E-Mail: cyberpublicationsdelhi@yahoo.com

WOMEN IN BUDDHIST TRADITION

Sameer Das Gupta

First Edition 2009

Published by :

G.S. Rawat for **Cyber Tech Publications**
4264/3, Ansari Road, Daryaganj, New Delhi-110002 (India)
Ph.: 011-23244078. Fax: 011-23280028
E-Mail: cyberpublicationsdelhi@yahoo.com

Printed at :

Preface

As Buddhism spread in ancient India, various Vinaya schools developed. Of the eighteen initial schools, three are extant today: the Theravada, which is widespread in Sri Lanka and Southeast Asia; the Dharmaguptaka, which is followed in Taiwan, China, Korea, and Vietnam; and the Mulasarvastivada, which is practiced in Tibet. All of these Vinaya schools have spread to Western countries in recent years. Considering that the Vinaya was passed down orally for many centuries before being written down and that the various schools had little communication with each other due to geographical distance, it is amazing that the monastic precepts are so consistent throughout. The differences among them are minor. Over the centuries, each school has developed its own ways of enumerating, interpreting, and living the precepts that accord with the culture and climate of that place.

In recent years, some women who hold eight- or ten-precept in countries where the bhikshuni sangha does not currently exist wish to receive that ordination. In 1996, ten Sri Lankan women received the bhikshuni ordination from a Korean sangha in India, and in 1998, over twenty Sri Lankan nuns received it in Bodhgaya, India, from Dharmaguptaka bhikshunis and Theravadin and Dharmaguptaka bhikshus. The bhikshuni ordination has subsequently been given several times in Sri Lanka, and while initially some Sri Lankan monks opposed this, some prominent monks supported it. Nowadays Theravadin bhikshunis, who number over 400, are accepted by Sri Lankan society.

—Author

CONTENTS

1

Women in Buddhism: An Introduction

INTRODUCTION

The position of women has been a subject of considerable interest in recent decades. In all societies, particularly in the West, there has been a rethinking of the position accorded to women in all spheres of activity. This has resulted in a significant change in the role played by women in social, economic and even political life. This reappraisal has also touched on the question of the position accorded to women in the main religious traditions of the world. In Christian countries the issue of the ordination of women has become a highly controversial topic, and some Churches are facing the prospect of dissension, and even schism, on this question. It is therefore opportune to consider the place accorded to women in Buddhism.

Sanghamittâ Day is particularly appropriate topic to reflect on concerning this question. This day, which falls on the full-moon day in the moth of Unduwap of the Sinhalese calendar (November-December in the Western one), is particularly important for Sri Lanka Buddhists. It marks the anniversary of the arrival of the Bhikkhuni Sanghamittâ, reputedly a daughter of the Emperor Asoka of ancient India, in Sri Lanka on a historic mission. Sanghamittâ brought with her two treasures. The first of these was the establishment of the Bhikkhuni Order in Sri Lanka, thus complementing the work of her brother Mahinda Thera who not only introduced the Order Bhikkhus into Sri Lanka but is also credited with the introduction of Buddhism itself to Sri Lanka.

The second of the treasures brought by Sanghamittâ was a sapling from the Bodhi tree under which the Buddha had attained enlightenment. It is ironic that whereas the Bhikkhuni Order (which because of its self- sustaining nature could have continued indefinitely) has disappeared in Sri Lanka, the Bodhi tree (a much more transient entity subject to the law of anicca) still flourishes in Sri Lanka. There is perhaps a lesson here on the difficulty of perpetuating a Buddhist institution which has to be based on human endeavor of a high quality, than in looking after and venerating a non-human object, which is unfortunately all too common with many Buddhists.

The role of women in Buddhism could be considered in several ways. We can, for instance, compare the position accorded to women in both the religious and the secular life in India before the Buddha's time with that after the establishment of Buddhism, and consider whether the Buddha's teaching resulted in a change radical or otherwise. We can see whether the Buddha's teaching accords to women a position different to that accorded to men, as is the case in many other religious. We may consider whether the accident of the sex of one's birth helps or retards progress on the Buddha's path, and indeed whether gender is itself a chance event or caused by pre-existing factors.

The part played by women in the early history of Buddhism, notably during the Buddha's own time, could be considered as providing a clue to the place accorded to women in Buddhism. In this connection the events surrounding the establishment of the Bhikkhuni Order need to be re-examined, as there is a measure of misunderstanding on this question. The influence of Buddhism on the position of women in the countries where Buddhism became a living presence could be highlighted. In this connection the significant facts pertaining to the mission of Sanghamittâ to Sri Lanka deserves notice. Finally the position of women in Buddhism could be contrasted with that accorded to women in the other great religious traditions of the modern world.

While the attitude of the Buddha to the role of women was an enlightened one, even when judged by the standards of the modern age, it must not be thought that everything that is said on this subject in Buddhist writing, even in the Pali Canon itself, measures up to the high standard expected of a Buddha. There are many explanations for this, not least of which is the fact that most of these works were written down several centuries after the Parinibbâna of the Buddha, and that during this time the teachings were sustained by monks, some of whom might not have been entirely free from the prejudices of the age. It is interesting to note that such "backsliding" occurs most commonly in the later works, e.g. in the prose sections of the Jataka (which incidentally are non-Canonical). And popular Buddhism took liberties of its own with this aspect of Buddhist teaching as it did with several others.

It is not possible to consider all these issues in a talk of this length. Only a few comments can be made on each of these questions. In particular it is not possible to comb the Buddhist texts to collect all the relevant issues relating to the position of women ill Buddhism. Fortunately this is not necessary as a small literature on this subject has accumulated since the late Ms I. B. Horner wrote her book Women under Primitive Buddhism well over 50 years ago. This book presents a comprehensive account of this question, and is still in may ways the best source on this question. But no apology is needed to revive this question at a time when the position of women in religious life is undergoing a critical re-examination in many places.

THE PRE-BUDDHIST POSITION OF WOMEN

The social matrix in which Buddhism arose was one which accorded to women an inferior position. In this regard Indian society did not differ radically from that in other places, and in some respects its treatment of women may actually have been more liberal. Indian religion in the Buddha's time is usually designated as "Brahmanism" to distinguish it from Hinduism, which in its classic form was a post-Buddhist development.

The position of women under Hinduism is well-known. Some idea of this position could be gleaned from the classic Hindu Dharmashâstras of which the Manu-smirthi, popularly knows as the "Laws of Manu", is the best known. This work describes the duties of women as follows"

> *"By a girl, by a young woman, or even by an aged one, nothing must be done independently, even in her own house. In childhood a female must be subject to her father, in youth to her husband, when her lord is dead to her sons; a woman must never be independent". (Laws of Manu, V, 147-8).*

Women were prevented from performing religious rites, and even the knowledge of the Vedas was to be kept away from them (IX, 18). The question for historians is how far these laws were in force at the time of the Buddha. The Hindus claim a divine origin for the laws of Manu, but they were probably complied later when Hinduism had assumed its rigid form centuries after the Buddha's time. However the Brahmanical religion of the Buddha's day, though somewhat better in this respect, did not accord spiritual parity to women. The primordial principle in the Vedic-Upanishadic philosophy which was dominant in the Buddha's time, was the male-principle (purusha), and this provided justification for the exclusion of women generally from social and spiritual activity.

It was in contrast to this attitude which reserved spiritual achievement for males that the Buddha proclaimed a message that was to be universal, one designed for the good of humanity as a whole without exception as to race, caste or sex. One of the classic titles given to the Buddha is "sattâ devamanussanam" or "teacher of gods and humans".

If the Buddha had been regarded as a teacher of men, as opposed to women the term "purisa" (which is the Pali counterpart of "itti", woman) would have been used in this classic description, rather than the generic term manussa. More generally the teaching of the Buddha is referred to as one that could lead all beings (sattâ) to liberation, in whatever realm they lived and whatever form they assumed.

However another of the classic description of the Buddha describes him as "Purisadammasârathi", or "charioteer of men to be tamed". Some might see in this sexist language, but what it probably means is precisely what it says, viz that men are subject to more violent misdeeds and have to be "tamed" to a greater extent than women.

While the change in attitude towards women brought about by the Buddha has to be appreciated it must be remembered that he was not alone in this regard.

The Jains too took a more enlightened attitude towards women when compared to the dominant Brâmanical religion. But Jainism unlike Buddhism did not concede the possibility of ultimate spiritual liberation to a woman, although a woman could become a man. Some, but not all, Jain sects extended their religious orders to women.

WOMEN AND THE BUDDHA'S PATH

There is very little, if any at all, in Buddhism that identifies it with a particular sex. The Buddha himself was historically a man, but the essence of Buddhism does not involve any extolling of the personality of the Buddha (unlike say the Christian extolling of the person of Jesus in his capacity as the Son of God). What the Buddha discovered was a universal law which existed independently of all the Buddhas, and which others, male or female, can discover by following the directions of the Buddha. The cult of the Buddha's person, the worship of relics, the conduct of the "Buddha pûjâs" and the like, were all later developments, both in the Theravada and the Mahayana, and have scant justification in the discourses of the Buddha.

Later academic speculation has raised the question whether a female could become a Buddha or a Bodhisattva. Mahayanists have taken an affirmative position (e.g. the cult of Kwan Yin as a Bodlihisattva who heeds the pleas of those in distress), but the Theravadan position is less clear. Some have claimed that the Buddhas have to be males, others have taken a more ambiguous position. The correct way to approach this question is to regard it as another of those profitless questions which the Buddha left unresolved (avyâkata), as it is irrelevant to the question of release from samsâra. There can be only one Buddha in a given Buddha-era (despite what some of the Jâtakas may imply), and the present era happened to have been inaugurated whether by necessity or coincidence, by a male, Siddhatta Gotama.

Another way to regard this question is that even though the male-female identity is set at birth, this is only true of a particular birth. The Buddhists doctrine of rebirth asserts that gender can change over successive transmigrations. Thus in the samsaric sense there is no male or female, but only a single karmic stream. This is hardly surprising given that the anattâ doctrine ensures that there is not even a persisting personal identity over the samsaric stream. This is another reason why the Dhamma for the most part ignores the sexual identity of persons.

Unfortunately a contrary view has gained some popularity in Buddhist countries, mainly due to the influence of the Jataka stories. In these stories men tend to be men and women tend to be women (e.g. Siddatta and Yasodarâ are said to have been consorts over countless births). As mentioned earlier, these stories are later accretions to the Buddhist tradition meant for popular consumption, and as we have them the essence of the stories seem to run counter to the fundamental Buddhist principle of anattâ. Only the stanzas in the Jatakas, which are bereft of narrative material, are considered canonical in the Theravada tradition. Another popular misunderstanding in many Buddhist countries is that negative ("unskillful") karma results in a man being reborn as a woman, and positive ("skillful") karma has the opposite effect. There does not seem to be any authoritative basis for this belief. In fact, the workings of the law of kamma is one of the unknowable questions for those who have not reached enlightenment. What factors result in a person becoming a male or a female were not discussed by the Buddha. Thus popular beliefs with regard to this are without foundation in the Buddha-dhamma.

On his deathbed the Buddha exhorted his followers to abide by the teaching, the Dhamma, which was to be the supreme guide. The Dhamma, of course, has no gender; the question is whether gender has anything to do with making the pursuit of the Path easy or difficult. The answer to this again is clear - the Buddha's path could be practiced by anyone, male or female. The eight components of the Noble Eight Fold Path are usually collected into three groups -

Sila or Morality, Bhâvanâ or spiritual growth, and Paññâ or Wisdom. The practice of morality may in some minor respects involve different kinds of conduct for the two sexes, but in the practice of the path gender has no relevance. The highest achievement of Buddhism, supreme enlightenment, is available to both men and women. This was stated categorically by the Buddha, well before there were any female Arahants, when he answered Ananda's question as to whether women could reach enlightenment in the affirmative. The point made here is so self- evident that it would not justify any more elaboration.

Buddhist practice, in its purest form, has no place for ritual. It is in the conducting of rituals in most religions that sex-typing becomes important and questions of precedence, ritual purity, and the like arise. Later developments in some Buddhist countries have seen the emergence of some rituals, but even this kind of simple rituals have not involved any typing by the sex of the devotee. Buddhist rituals usually involves simple forms of worship, chanting or symbolic offerings, and all of these are available for men and women on equal terms.

In this connection it must also be mentioned that Buddhism has no place for a priestly class. Buddhist monks are sometimes mistakenly referred to as "Buddhist priests", but this is wrong use of terminology and should be avoided by all Buddhists. The role of the priest in religious life is to officiate between the faithful and the God , and Buddhism being essentially atheistic, has no place for a God or priest. Thus Buddhism has been spared the problem now all too evident ill theistic religions of women protesting their exclusion from the priestly circle. The position of monks and nuns in Buddhism will be considered in a later section.

The disciples of the Buddha, especially the more perceptive of the female followers, appear to have grasped very well the principle that the Dhamma was neutral with respect to the gender of the person following its dictates. There are not many direct references to this question, but an incident reported twice in the Sutta Pitaka is very relevant to this and must be considered.

This records the taunt of Mara to the Theri Soma that no woman could reach "the high ground of the wise" because she has only the "two-finger knowledge (dvangulapaññâ)", an allusion to cooking where the consistency of the cooked rice is tested by pressing it between the fingers. The refutation of Mâra, as given hi the Sanyutta Nikâya, is worth quoting in full:

ittibhâvo kim kiyirâ *cittamhi susamâhite* *ñânamhi vattamânamhi* *sammâdhamma.m vipassato*	What matters being a woman If with mind firmly set One grows in the knowledge Of the Right Law, with insight?
yassa nûna siyâ eva itthâham puriso ti va kiñci va pana asamîti tam Maro vattum arahatîti	Any one who has to question Am I a woman or am I a man And does not oneself really know Over such a one will Mara triumph

The version given in the Therigâthâ preserves the essential first stanza which asserts the irrelevance of the "female condition" (ittibhâvo) to spiritual progress, but replaces the second with a more conventional stanza:

sabbattha vihatâ nanadi tamokkhadho padâlito evam janâhi pâpima nihato tvam asi antaka	With pleasures overcome everywhere And the mass of ignorance torn away Know this, 0 Defiled One, Driven out art thou at last!

Whether this involves some later reworking by monk compilers we shall never know. It is however a fact that the udânas recorded in the Therigâtha are somewhat disappointing if we were to look in them for evidence on the question that is considered here. In most respects what the Theris see as the travails of life from which they seek escape into the ineffable, are not different from those identified by the theras in the Theragâthâ.

THE SECULAR POSITION OF WOMEN IN BUDDHISM

When we consider the position accorded to women in ordinary life we have to note that the Buddha's teaching was primarily concerned with individual spiritual emancipation. This emancipation would be manifested in the worldly conduct of individuals, but the Buddha was not interested in establishing and perpetuating a particular worldly order, for whatever actual regime that would be put in place would in a Buddhist sense be unsatisfactory. In this respect Buddhism differs from other religions where private and public affairs were brought within the gambit of religious regulation.

Thus Buddhism does not take such things as marriage (where the position of women is important) as a religious "sacrament".. as it is, for instance, in Christianity or Hinduism. The Buddhist position was that these matters have to be regulated by society thorough some kind of social, political or legal process. It is only required that such arrangements should not be in fundamental conflict with the Dhamma. It is possible to have many different kinds of social and family arrangements which are compatible with the broad framework of the Dhamma. Thus matters like divorce, inheritance of property, etc. are entirely regulated by social processes, and there is considerable freedom for individuals in these arrangements.

In matters like marriage, divorce, ownership of property, personal political or religious beliefs, etc. wives were allowed considerable liberty, and this was something that was to astonish Christian missionaries to Buddhist countries.

Nonetheless in his discourses to the lay person the Buddha does express views, and recommend practices which he considered as compatible with the Dhamma. Sometimes the Buddha's views happened to coincide with commonly accepted social principles, sometimes they were contrary to these views.

Thus for instance, in a society which considered male children to be more desirable than female ones, the Buddha held a different view. When King Pasenadi of Kosala, while still an adherent of the Brahmanical religion and thus shared its values, was disappointed that his Queen Mallika bore him a daughter, the Buddha told him: "A woman-child, 0 Lord of men, may prove to be a better offspring than a male" (San. Nik, iii, 2, 6). It is possible to see in this a kind of diplomatic response to prevent the King developing an aversion to his Queen who was a Buddhist, but the sentiment expressed is genuine, and in keeping with the rest of the Buddha's teaching.

A few discourses given to householders emphasize the more worldly aspects of living, and of these the Sigalovada Sutta is the best known. This Sutta has been dissected to get actual rules of conduct on a wide variety of secular matters. This is a wrong way to approach the question. In this Sutta the Buddha was not laying down a code of domestic jurisprudence but instructing the Brahmin Sigala on certain basic principles. Of these the ones that are relevant here are the duties of wife to husband and vice versa. The Buddha lays down rules in this regard that could be considered common sense and eminently sensible. They conform to the mores of the time. The actual details are not important, but what is important is that the Buddha emphasizes the principle of reciprocity. Thus just as the wife has duties prescribed vis-a-vis the husband, so has the husband towards the wife.

The equal burden of responsibility and duty laid on both husband and wife is the hall-mark of the Buddha's attitude to the role of women in the family life. In this Sutta the Buddha identifies qualities in women (beauty, wealth, kin, sons, virtue) which would make them the superior partner in a marriage, but these qualities are those generally accepted in society in the Buddha's time. The Sigalovada Sutta presupposes a monogamous system, but some of the royal patrons of the Buddha practiced polygamy having large harems, but they were not admonished for this by the Buddha. This was a matter belonging to social convention, and the Buddha preferred not to pontificate on it.

At other places in the Pali Canon there are references to the position of females that might not satisfy a modern exponent of "women's liberation". Thus the Dhaniya Sutta of the Sutta Nipata extols obedience in wives (reminding us of the Christian marriage vow imposed on wives to "obey" their husbands). Then there are the various lists of kinds of wives that appear in the Vinaya and the Sutta Pitaka, with the occasional hint that the more docile the kind of wife the better. But it must be remembered that these opinions do not have any kind of binding force, and are not always consistent with statements elsewhere. In a compilation as large as the Pali Canon such inconsistency on relatively minor matter is to be expected.

If one were to get a general principle on the question of the relation between the sexes it is the principle of reciprocity and non-dominance that emerges in the Buddhist writing. Even in the later Jatakas it is sometimes stated that woman who live in fear of their husbands are not true wives (No.537).

THE ORDER OF BHIKKHUNIS

This is often regarded as crucial to the evaluation of the role of women in Buddhism. What can be concluded is that while Buddhism passes this test it does so with a few minor qualifications. Every religion has jealously guarded entry into its innermost sanctum. In many religions the doors of this sanctum are barred to women. In Buddhism one could consider the Sangha as forming part of the core of the Buddha Sâsana (Dispensation of the Buddha). It is part of the Triple Gem to which all Buddhists go for refuge. There is some argument as to whether the Sangha consists of those who have formally undertaken to follow the rules of the Vinaya, or consists of those who have "entered the stream" be they monk or lay, but we shall not consider this questions here, and take the popular view that the Sangha consists of the former.

As is well-known that the Buddha established the Order for Bhikkhus a few months after his enlightenment, and established the Bhikkhuni Order only five years later. The facts relating to the establishment of the Bhikkhuni Order are well known and need not be recounted here in full. We have Maha Prajapati G6tami, the foster mother of the Buddha, expressing her wish to enter the Order; we hear of the Buddha's rejection of this request; we see Prajâpati Gotami persisting in her request, and even following the Buddha over long distances; we then hear of Ananda's pleas to the Buddha on her behalf; and we have the Buddha's final consent.

The establishment of the Bhikkhu Order is considered as something revolutionary in religious history. It is the first time that we have a body of men coming under a strict discipline not discharging a priestly function, all earnestly engaged in seeking a way of release. Previously ascetics were individual wanderers (samanas), not belonging to a body corporate. The Jains are sometimes credited with first establishing a religious Order but the Jain orders were something intermediate between the isolated Hindu ascetic and the organized body of samanas that constituted the Bhikkliu Sangha. The extension of the monastic principle to women was even more revolutionary. Involvement of women in the religious life has at most times been either non-existent or dubious (as for instance in the case of the

Indian devadasis and their counterparts in other countries). In course of time Prajâpati Gotami's wish to become a Bhikkhuni became the common aspiration of many women. Perhaps they saw in the Bhikkhuni order a freedom that they could not find in the secular life, where they were bound down by the rules of a society which accorded little importance to women.

The Buddha's decision to sanction the establishment of an Order for women in the fifth year after his enlightenment was a landmark in Buddhist and Indian history. But by the standards of the modern age it was marred by the special rules which the Buddha imposed on the Bhikkhunis. Thus Prajâpati Gotami had to agree to 8 special rules (garudhammâ) before she was ordained, and these rules were later incorporated in the Bhikkhuni Vinaya. These rules could be summarized as follows:

1. Bhikkhus were always to have precedence over Bhikkhunis in matters of salutation, etc. irrespective of any other consideration.
2. Bhikkhunis could not observe the annual retreat (vassa) in a district where there were no Bhikkhus.
3. Bhikkhus had to set the dates for Bhikkhuni Uposatha ceremonies.
4. Confessing transgressions by Bhikkhnis had to done before the assembly of both Bhikkhus and Bhikkhunis.
5. Certain judicial processes in case of Bhikkhunis had to be undertaken by both the Sanghas.
6. Upasampadâ initiation of Bhikkhunis should be given by the Bhikkhu sangha as well.
7. A Bhikkhuni should never abuse a Bhikkhu.
8. Bhikkhus can officially admonish Bhikkhunis, but not vice versa

That these rules involve a subordination of Bhikkhunis to Bhikkhus cannot be denied. Some of the rules may be explained in terms of practical necessity. Thus Rule 2 recognized the dangers to which Bhikkhunis would be exposed to if they spent the long period of retreat in isolated areas. Rules 3 and 6 might have been set up to see that the procedures in the newly established Bhikkhuni Order would correspond to and benefit from similar procedures in the already established Bhikkhu Sangha. Rule 7 seems to be a restatement of the precept regarding "wrong speech". But Rules 1 and 8 cannot be seen in any other light than a concession to male superiority.

In practical terms Rule 1 must have been the most irksome, and even humiliating in a society where the protocol attaching to salutation was very strict. The usual Buddhist rule which guided seniority was the number of years a person had spent in the Order, and while this continued to apply to Bhikkhus and Bhikkhnis considered separately, any individual Bhikkhuni had always to pay respect to any Bhikkhu however junior the latter may have been. It is not surprising that it was from this rule that Prajâpati Gotami sought exemption (unsuccessfully despite the support of Ananda). Yet whatever be the explanation the rules lack reciprocity between males and females, and would not suit the present age. Unfortunately the extinction of the Order of Bhikkhunis must mean that this question has to remain an academic one. On his deathbed the Buddha gave permission to revise the less important rules of the Vinaya, but the offer was never taken. Whether this contributed to the extinction of the Bhikkhuni Order we shall never know. A few more comments will be made in connection with Sanghamittâ and Sri Lankan Buddhism.

The special rules for Bhikkhunis have come for criticism from certain Western observers. In Christianity there were no female priests, and therefore no equivalent to Bhikkhunis.

The closest that we have are the various orders of Christian nuns (whose equivalents in Buddhist countries are the women who-take the ten precepts). The position of Christian nuns vis-a-vis monks and male laity is distinctly worse that the position of Bhikkhunis under the Vinaya rules. At least the Bhikkhunis did not have to acknowledge (after the death of the Buddha) a male person as the spiritual head (as for instance Christian nuns would have to acknowledge the Pope or the Bishop).

The subordination of Bhikkhunis to Bhikkhus could be seen as one relating to protocol rather than to spiritual progress. Even amongst monks it does not follow that a more senior monk is necessarily more spiritually advanced than another who is a junior in terms of years spent in the Order. Similarly while Bhikkhunis may rank lower than Bhikkhus in terms of formal position they can be more advanced in terms of spiritual attainment.

WOMEN IN EARLY BUDDHISM

Once the order of Bhikkhunis was founded a large number of distinguished women from various social backgrounds came to adorn this Order, attracted by the power of the Buddha's teaching and the freedom which the new Order offered them. Many of these Bhikkhunis attained to the supreme bliss of enlightenment. The stories, sayings and deeds of these distinguished Bhikkhunis are recorded in many places in the Pali Canon, most notably in the Therigâtha, a compilation of verses uttered by these Theris when they saw the clear light of the Dhamma, and which constitutes a part of the Khuddaka Nikaya of the Sutta Pitaka.

Amongst those in the Udâna are recorded in the Therigâthâ are some of the best known names in early Buddhism. The include Prajâpati Gotami, who was the first

Bhikkhuni, Uppalavannâ and Khema, who are traditionally regarded as "foremost of the Bhikkhunis", Kisâgotami and Patacâra, who figure in the best known stories in early Buddhism. The members of the order belonged to all walks of life. Some were former courtesans like Ambapâli and Vimala, others were of royal lineage like Sumeda and Sela. There were distinguished exponents of he Dhamma like Dhammadinnâ, scions of noble or merchant families like Bhadda Kundalkesa, Sujâta, and Anopama, not to mention those of humbler origins like Punnika the slave girl, or Chanda the daughter of a poor Brahmin. The actual numbers of Theris involved is not known. Patacâra is credited with having 500 personal followers, and there are several unnamed Thens to whom sayings are attributed.

The accomplishment of these Theris of old is that they gave living proof of the Buddha's utterance (Sam.Nik., 1, 5, 6):

yassa etâdisa.m yâna.m *ittiyâ purisassa va* *sa ve etena yânena* *nibbanasseva santike ti*	This is the only vehicle Be it a woman or be it a man The one who takes this vehicle Can reach the peace of Nibbâna

where the chariot referred to is the Buddha-Dhamma.

Apart from these Theris and Arahants there were many women from all walks of life who embraced the Buddha's teaching. They became upâsikâs and sâvakas, students and servitors of the Buddha and the Sangha. Their names have gone down in Buddhist legend and their piety is well known. These stories do not need repetition here.

CONCLUSION

By way of conclusion we may reflect on the heritage of Sanghamittâ and compare the Buddhist position on the role of women in religious life with that of the other dominant religions.

However strong was the role of women in the Buddha's day once the charismatic presence of the Buddha ended with his death, the-Bhikkhuni sangha too appeared to have entered into decline. While the Bhikkhu Sangha has continued in unbroken succession in many parts of the world (though not in the land of its birth) the fate of the Bhikkhuni Sanglia is less well recorded.

The Buddha is credited with the prophecy that the lifespan of the Buddha Sâsana would be curtailed because of the creation of the Bhikkhuni order. Whatever value be added to such prophecies, it is a fact that after the period foreseen by the Buddha (500 years) Buddhism saw the great bifurcation between the Mahayana and the Theravada streams. Even the Theravada which is the closest of these two streams to the original views of the Buddha, developed numerous tendencies which were not seen in the Buddha's day. The rise of the Mahayana has had some implications for the role of women in Buddhism. It has been claimed that the Mahayana entertained a more positive attitude toward the role of women than the Theravada. However, the early Mahayana masters were all male. Indeed it is the claim of some Mahayana sects that the Buddha established a line of patriarchs with Maha Kassapa as the first. This line of patriarchs naturally all consisted of males. When Chinese orders of Bhikshunis were finally established this was done with the aid of Theravada bhikkhunis from Sri Lanka.

While the Mahayana bhikshuni orders still survive the fate of the bhikkhuni order in Theravada countries has been different. In India itself not only the bhikkhuni order but also the bhikkhu order came to an end. But before this happened both orders were established in Sri Lanka which henceforth became the source of Theravada Buddhism. There is no evidence that a Theravada bhikkhuni order has existed in any country other than India and Sri Lanka. Whereas the Bhikkhu order was exported to countries in South-East

Asia this does not seem to have been the case with the Bhikkhuni Order.

Sanghamitta's role in bringing the Bhikkhuni Order to Sri Lanka has been noted earlier. She seems to have had a great initial success with many of the leading ladies of the country including those of royal blood taking to the monastic life. From Sri Lanka the Bhikkhuni Sangha was taken to China in the fifth century by enterprising Sri Lankan Bhikkhunis. Other than this very little is recorded of the activity of Bhikkhunis in Sri Lanka. We do not even have the exact date as to when the Order vanished in Sri Lanka. This also meant the extinction of the Theravada Bhikkhuni order in the current dispensation of Gotama.

The question for the modern age is whether the Bhikkhuni order should be revived, and if so how this could be done. In Sri Lanka and other Theravada countries women who want to play a more active role than that of lay followers of the Dhamma can only take the Ten Precepts .

The dominant opinion amongst the Sangha in Theravada countries is that there is no possibility of resuscitating the Bhikkhuni Order. This follows from the traditional requirement of an appropriate lineage for the perpetuation of a particular Order. Thus Bhikkhunis have to be ordained by other Senior Bhikkhunis although the Vinaya also requires the participation of Bhikkhus. Those who argue for the revival of the Bhikkhuni Order argue that technically the lineage of Sanghamitta Theri still continues to flourish in a few places where Chinese Buddhism still flourishes. True, the Mahayana practices differ from those in the Theravada. But if the technical requirement of an unbroken lineage is what is needed to revive the Bhikkhuni Order a way could be found by using this curious survival of the heritage of Sanghamitta Theri in a foreign land. But that Bhikkhus must also participate and the conjunction of

Mahayana Bhikshunis with Theravada Bhikkhus to re-establish a Theravada Bhikkhuni Order will run into serious difficulty from both sides.-

But even without a Bhikkhuni order there is ample scope for the participation of women in Dhamma work. The Buddha has not said that enlightenment can come only from formal adherence to a monastic order. Both laymen and laywomen have become arahants in the past. Thus the door to the highest goal of Buddhism is not barred to women simply because the Bhikkhuni order has become extinct.

A few comments of the Buddhist position of women with that of other religions may be made. We have had occasion to make a few remarks on the position of women under classic Hinduism. Modern Hinduism has not changed much, although there has been some elevation in the social position of women. Women cannot still officiate as priests ill the Hindu religion.

Christianity has traditiotially been a masculine religion mainly because its main dogma relates to a God considered as a male ("Father") and a prophet-teacher Jesus who is considered as his "Son". The centerpiece of the religion is the Father-Son relationship, and it is not surprising that women have been relegated to a secondary place and denied spiritual equality with men. Jesus considered himself to be a Jewish Messiah, and did not challenge Jewish views on this subject. His comments on the role of women are at best ambiguous. None of the 12 original disciples were women.

The modern Christian Church was constituted out of the claims of Jesus by St Peter, who is well-known as a misogynist, and the subsequent record of Christian Churches has reflected this quite well. Now there are moves to ordain women priests in some Christian denominations but these moves have led to much dissension.

The position of women in Islam is well known. They too are denied full access to religious functions, and in some countries even access to the mosque. It is disturbing that the revival of Islamic fundamentalism is threatening to undo some progress that has been made in some Islamic countries.

Thus whatever comparison we may care to make with other religions the Buddhist view on this question is not only enlightening but unique.

Of all Buddhist tales, the best-known and best-loved is the story of Buddha's own birth and youth. Buddha-"the Enlightened One" or "The Awakened One"-is the religious title given to Siddhartha Gautama, a prince of the Sakya clan, which ruled an area that today straddles the border between Nepal and the Indian state of Bihar. He is believed to have lived from around 563 to around 483 B.C.

No official account of Buddha's life was left by either Buddha or his disciples. As with most great religious leaders, the stories of his early life were gradually expanded and embellished by his followers. Still, the legend probably represents in symbolic form the early spiritual life of the young man who became the Buddha.

In the royal city of Kapilavatthu, a son had come to the great King Suddhodana and his lovely Queen Maya. They named the boy Siddhartha, which means "He Who Reaches His Goal."

Soon after the birth, the king was visited by a great seer named Asita. The baby was brought for him to see. To the king's alarm, the holy man burst into tears.

"Sir, what is wrong?" asked the king. "Do you foresee some disaster for my son?"

"Not at all," said the seer. "His future is supreme. Your son shall become a Buddha, an Enlightened One, and free the world from its bonds of illusion. I weep only for myself, for I will not live to hear his teachings."

Now, the king was distressed that his only heir might turn to a life of religion. He called upon eight Brahmin priests, all skilled in interpreting signs, and asked them to prophesy for the prince.

When the priests had conferred, their spokesman addressed the king. "Your majesty, if your son follows in your footsteps, he will become a Universal King and rule the known world. But if he renounces home and family for the life of a seeker, he will become a Buddha and save the world from its ignorance and folly."

The king asked, "What would cause my son to renounce home and family?"

The priest answered, "Seeing the four signs."

"And what are the four?"

"An old man, a sick man, a dead man, and a holy man."

"Then none of these shall he see," the king declared. And he placed guards around the palace to keep all such persons away.

As Siddhartha grew to manhood, the king sought ways to strengthen the prince's ties to home. He married him to the lovely Princess Yasodhara, who in time bore a son. And he surrounded him with dancing girls to while away his hours. The prince became a creature of pleasure and seldom left his luxurious apartments in the palace's upper stories.

But one day Siddhartha thought he would visit a park outside the city. The king arranged the outing, with strict orders to his guards to keep the road clear of the old, the sick, the dead, and the holy.

As the prince passed through the city in his royal carriage, people lined the road to admire him. The guards followed the king's orders as best they could. But even so, the prince spied in the crowd a man with gray hair, weak limbs, and bent back.

"Driver," said Siddhartha, "what is wrong with that man?"

"He is old, my lord."

"And what is 'old'?" asked the prince.

"'Old' is when you have lived many years."

"And will I too become 'old'?"

"Yes, my lord. To grow old is our common fate."

"If all must face old age," said the prince, "then how can we take joy in youth?"

Not long after, the prince spied a man yellow-faced and shaking, leaning on a companion for support. "Driver, what is wrong with that man?"

"He is sick, my lord.

"And what is 'sick'?"

"'Sick' is when your health has left you."

"And will I too become 'sick'?"

"It is likely, my lord. To be sick is our common fate."

"If all must face sickness," said the prince, "then how can we take pride in health?"

Before long, the prince spied a stiff, motionless man being carried along by four others.

"Driver, what is wrong with that man?"

"He has died, my lord."

"And what is 'die'?"

"'Die' is when your life is finished."

"And will I too 'die'?"

"You will, my lord, without a doubt. Of all our fates, death is the most certain."

"If all must face death," said the prince, "then how can we delight in life?"

At last the prince spied a man with shaved head and saffron robe.

"Driver, what is that man."

"He is a seeker, my lord."

"And what is a 'seeker'?"

"A 'seeker' is one who renounces home and family to wander about, living on what he begs. Avoiding pleasure, he subdues the passions; meditating, he controls the mind. And so he strives for freedom from this world of tears and the endless round of rebirths."

"Driver, return to the palace. No more do I care for parks or pleasure or anything that may pass away. Soon I too will be a seeker, renouncing this life that binds me."

That very night, Siddhartha slipped into the women's quarters for one last look at his sleeping wife and son. Then quietly he descended to the courtyard, mounted a white steed, and set out.

The city gate, too heavy for a single man, swung open by itself at his approach. And as the prince passed through, he made this vow:

"Never shall I enter this city again, till I've seen the farther shore of life and death."

2

Gaining an Immediate Reward for Faith in the Three Treasures

Lord Otomo no Yasunoko no muraji of the Great Flower Rank was an ancestor of the Otomo no muraji in Uji, Nagusa district, Kii province. He was endowed with a lucid mind and highly revered the Three Treasures.

According to a record, in the reign of Emporer Bitatsu, sounds of musical instruments were heard off the coast of Izumi province. They sounded like pipes and strings or rolling thunder. They were heard in the daytime and at night a light spread estward. Lord Otomo no Yasunoko no muraji heard this tale and reported it to the emporer, who did not believe it and remained silent. When he reported it to the empress, however, she ordered him to investigate. He went to the seaside to witness the scene and found it exactly as reported. While there, he came upon a camphor log which had been struck by thunder. On his return, he said to the empress, "I have found a camphor log on the beach of Takaashi. I humbly request permission to make Buddha images out of it." The empress gave permission saying, "Your wish is granted."

Yasunoko was very happy and announced the imperial decree to Shima no oomi, who, in great joy, commissioned

Ikeba no atae Hita to carve three bodhisattvas. They were consecrated in a hall at Toyura to inspire awe and reverence in the people. However, Lord Mononobe no yuge no Motiya no omuraji address the empress, saying, "NO Buddha images should be kept in this country.

They must be thrown away." Hearing this, the empress call Lord Ysaunoko no muraji, saying, "Hide these Buddha images without delay." Thereupon he had Hita no atae hide them among rice sheaves. Lord Yuge no omuraji eventually burned the hall and threw the remaining images into the canal at Naniwa. He rebuked Yasunoko, saying, "The cause of our present disaster lies in keeping pagan images sent from a neighboring country. Give them up and throw them into the current which flows toward Korea." ("Pagan images" mean "Buddha images.") Yasunoko firmly refused. Yuge no omuraji, deranged and rebellious, looked for an opportunity for treason, but heaven disliked him and earth heatedhim. He was at last overthrown in the reign of Emporer Yomei, and the Buddhist images were brought into the open to be kept for posterity. The image of Amida is now enshrined at Hiso-dera at Yoshino.

In the first month in he spring of the tenth year of the ox, the empress was enthroned at the Palace of Owarida, and reigned for thirty-six years. On the tenth of the fourth month, in the summer of the first year of her reign, Prince Umayado was appointed Prince Regent, and Yasunoko no muraji was made his personal attendant.

On the fifth of the fifth month of the thirteenthyear of th ereign, the empress gave him the Great Fifth Fank, saying, "Your distinuished service shall be remembered forever." In the second month of the seventeenth year, the Prince Regent entrusted him with six hundred and seventy acres of rice fields at Iho district in Harima province. When the Prince Regent died at the Palace if Ikaruga in the secondmonth of the twenty-ninth year, Yasunoko no muraji revealed his desire to renounce the world, but the empress did not permit this.

In the fourth month of the thrity-second year, a Buddhist monk took an axe and smote his father with it. Yasunoko no muraji immediately petitioned the throne, saying, "All monks and nuns should be examind and a presiding officer appointed in order to guide them and establish righteousness." The empress agreed and granted him the right to carry out the task. It turned out there were eight hundred and thirty-seven monks and five hundred and seventy-nine nuns. The monks Kanroku was appointed daisojo, and Yasunoko no muraji and Kuratsukuri no Tokosaka were appointed sozu.

On the eighth of the tenth month of the thirty-third year, Yasunoko died suddenly at Naniwa, His corpse was unusually fragrant, and the empress declared seven days' mourning in honor of his loyalty. He returned to life in three days, however, and told his family the following tale: "There were five-colored clouds like a rainbow stretching to the north. I was walking along that roadway of clouds, and it smelled fragrant, as if valuable incense was being mixed. At the end of the way there appeared a golden maountain which dazzled my eyes as I approached it. There the late Prince Shotoku was waiting for me and we climbed to the summit together. A full-fledged monk was standing on the top of the golden mountain. Bowing to the prince, he said, 'I have come from the Palace in the East. In eight days you will fall into danger. I beseech you to take this elixir of life.' Then he gave one bead of his bracelet to be swallowed, and, with the penetrating eye, he had the prince recite three times, 'Homage to the Bodhisattva of Miraculous Powers' and retired. The prince said to me, 'Go back home without delay and prepare a place to make a Buddha statue. When I finish performing the rite of repentence, I will return to the court to make it.' I cam back along the way I had taken before, and all of a sudden I was brought back to life."

Accordingly, people called him the "Revived Muraji." In the ninth month in the autumn of the seventh year of the dog, the sixth year of the reign of Emporer Kotoku, he was decorated with the Great Flower Rank, Upper Grade, and when he died he was overy ninety.

A note says: How praiseworthy the member of the Otomo family is for his devotion to Buddha, for his commitment to dharma with purity of heart and loyalty, and for his longevity and fortune! He was known for his courage, and for the sense of filial piety he handed down to his descendants. Indeed we know it is a testimony to the Three Treasures, and it is due to protection by good deities. On reflection we discover that danger in eight days corresponds to eight years; "Bodhisattva of Miraculous Power" corresponds to Bodhisattva Monjushiri, the "one bead" which was swallowed is a pill to escape danger. "The golden mountain" is identified with Wu-t'ai-shan in China, while the "Palace of the East" means Japan. The "going back to the court to make an image" was realized in the birth of ex-Emporer Shoho-ojin-shomu, who built a temple and Buddha Statue. The Most Venerable Gyogi, a contemporary of Emporer Shomu, is an incarnation of Bodhisattva Monjushiri. This is a miraculous story.

GAINING AN IMMEDIATE REWARD FOR FAITH IN BODHISATTVA KANNON

Elder Master Gyozen came from the Katashibe family and was sent to Koryo for Buddhist studies during the reign of the empress who resided at the Palace of Owarida. When that country was invaded, he wandered from place to place. When he came to a river, he was at a loss how to cross it, for there was neither bridge nor boat. Sitting on a broken-down bridge, he was meditating on Kannon when an old man came by in a boat to take him to the other side. Upon landing, he could see neither the old man nor the boat. Thus he learned that the old man was an incarnation of Kannon; and on the spot he made a vow that he would make an image to be venerated.

Eventually he reached Great T'ang China where he made an image to worship day and night. He was called Dharma Master Riverside. No one exceeded him in fortitude, and he was respected by the emporer of the T'ang dynasty. He returned home with the Japanese envoys to China in the second year of the Yoro era. He lived at Kofuku-ji and never ceased performing services before that image until he died. Surely we learn that the power of Kannon is beyond understanding. The note says: An eminent monk went to study abroad, fell into danger, and was unable to cross at the ferry. On a bridge he meditated on Kannon and trusted holy power. Kannon, in the form of an old man, came to his rescue and disappeared after they had parted. The monk made an image of Kannon and worshiped it continuously until his last day.

PAYING FOR AND FREEING TURTLES AND BEING REWARDED IMMEDIATELY AND SAVED BY THEM

Dhyana Master Gusai came from Paekche, when that country was invaded, an ancestor of the governor of Mitami district in Bingo province was put in charge of reinforcements and sent to Paekche. At that time the present governor's ancestor vowed that he would build a temple to dedicate to the deities of heaven and earth if he came home safely. Eventually, he escaped harm. Thereupon, he invited Dhyana Master Gusai to return to Japan with him. Mitani-dera is the temple that was founded by this master, and both monks and laymen felt awe and reverence at its sight. Once, in going to the capital to exchange his belongings for gold and paints, the master reached the port of Naniwa. He happened to sea a seaman selling four big turtles, and he advised people to buy them and set them free. After that he rented a boat and boarded it with two acolytes to cross the sea. Late at night, the sailors, filled with greed, threw the acolytes into the sea near Kabanejima, in Bizen, and turned to him saying, "Quick, into the sea with you!" The monk tried to reason with them, but they would not listen. Finally, after making a vow, he sank into the water. When the water came up to his waist, he felt a stone supporting his legs. In the morning light he found that he was being carried by the turtles. They left him on the beach of Bitchu after nodding to him three times. It seems that the turtles which had been set free came back to repay his kindness.

Eventually the thieving sailors, six in all, happened to visit his temple to sell the gold and paints they had stolen from him. The patron of the temple first came out to make an estimate, and then the master appeared to see them. The thieves were petrified with terror. Out of mercy he did not punish them, but rather made a Buddha image to be consecrated in the pagoda and performed rites of dedication. Later he lived by the seaside, and preached to passersby. He passed away when he was over eighty.

Even an animal does not forget gratitude, and repays an act of kindness. How, then, could a righteous man fail to have a sense of gratitude?

A DEAF MAN WHOSE HEARING WAS RESTORED IMMEDIATELY OWING TO HIS FAITH IN A MAHAYANA SCRIPTURE

In the reign of the empress residing at the Palace of Owarida there was a man whose name was Kinunui no tomonomiyatsuko Gitsu who suddenly became seriously ill. He was deaf in both ears and suffered a chronic skin disease which never healed. He said to himself, "My past deeds influence my life not only in the present but also in the future. It is better to do good and die soon than to live long and be hated by others." Therefore he swept the ground, cleaned the hall, summoned the dhyana master with all due reverence, and, after purifying himself with holy water, devoted himself to reading a Mahayana scripture.

Meanwhile, he experienced an extraordinary sensation and said to the master, "I am hearing the name of a bodhisattva in my ear, so I beg you, Most Venerable Master, to continue the service." During the master's performance, one ear was completely healed. With great joy, Gitsu repeated his request to go on, and, as the master went on with the service, both ears were healed. People far and near marveled at the news. We learn that there really exists a mysterious correspondence.

A WOMAN WHO PERFORMED WORK IN AN EXTRAORDINARY WAY, ATE SACRED HERBS, AND FLEW UP TO HEAVEN ALIVE

In the fifth year of the Hakuchi era of the emporer who resided at the Palace of Nagara no Toyosaki in Naniwa, heavenly beings communicated with her, and she ate special herbs gathered in the field in springtime and flew about in the heavens. Indeed, we know that her extraordinary qualities and her diet of special herbs are well recognized, even though she has not studied Buddhist teachings. The Shojin nyomon-kyo gives this relevant passage: "You will be able to achieve five kinds of merit by leading a lay life and sweeping the garden with an upright mind."

RECOLLECTING AND RECITING THE HOKE-KYO AND GAINING AN IMMEDIATE REWARD TO SHOW AN EXTRAORDINARY SIGN

In Kazuraki upper district, Yamato province, there was once a devotee of the Hoke-kyo. He came from the Tajihi family, and, even before he was eight years old, he could recite the Hoke-kyo with the exception of one character which always escaped his memory and continued to escape it even when he was in his twenties. Setting forth on his quest, he reached Saru's home at last and knocked at the door. A woman came and reported back to her mistress with a smile, saying, "There is a guest at the door who looks exactly like your deceased son." On hearing this, the mistress went to the door to see the guest, finding him the very image of her deceased son.

In wonder, the master asked the guest, "Who are you?" And the latter answered by announcing the name of his home district and province. In turn, the guest asked the same question, and he was given a detailed answer. It became evident to him that they were his parents in his former life. He knelt down to pay respect to them. Saru affectionately invited him into the house, and, staring at him as he sat in the seat of honor, said, "Aren't you the spirit of my deceased son?" Their guest told them in detail about his dream and announced that the old couple were his parents. Saru, after some reminiscing, motioned to him, saying, "My late son, so and so, lived in this hall, read this scripture, and used this pitcher."

The son entered the hall, opened the scripture, and found that the character which he could never remember was missing, for it had been burned with a lamp. When the yound man repented of his offense and repaired the text, he could recite it correctly. Parents and son were amazed and delighted, and the son never lost the parent-child relationship and his sense of filial piety.

The note says: How happy is this member of the Kusakabe family who, in pursuit of the path through Buddhist scripture, recited the Hoke-kyo in two lives, present and past, and served two fathers to be renowned in posterity.

It is an extraordinary phenomenon, and not commonplace. Indeed, we are sure it is due to the divine influence of the Hoke-kyo and the miraculous power of Kannon. In the same spirit, the Zen'aku ingo-kyo says, "Look at present effects if you want to know past causes. Look at present deeds if you want to know future effects."

RIDICULING A RECITER OF THE HOKE-KYO AND GETTING A TWISTED MOUTH AS AN IMMEDIATE PENALTY

In Yamashiro province there was once a self-ordained novice whose name is unknown. He used to play go all the time. One day when he was playing go with a layman, a mendicant came to recite the Hoke-kyo and beg for alms. The novice laughed at him, mimicking his accent with a twisted mouth. The laymen was greatly shocked at this and exclaimed, "How awful!" at each turn of the game. The layman won the game every time, and the novice lost. Meanwhile the novice's mouth became twisted, and no medicine could cure it. The gist of this story is stated in the Hoke-kyo as follows: "Those who laugh at and slight this scripture will lose many teeth and get a twisted mouth, a flattened nose, crippled limbs and squint eyes." It is better to be possessed by evil spirits and talk in a daze than to abuse the devotees of the Hoke-kyo. Remember that evil comes from one's mouth.

SHOWING AN EXTRAORDINARY SIGN AT THE MOMENT OF DEATH OWING TO DEVOTION TO BUDDHIST STUDIES AND SPREADING THE TEACHING FOR THE BENEFIT OF ALL BEINGS

The late Dharma Master Dosho belonged to the Fune family in Kawachi province. Under the emporer's auspices he went abroad for Buddhist studies to T'ang China, where he met and studied with Hsuan-tsang san-tsang. This master said to his other disciples, "This man will teach many on his return home. You should not slight him but guide him well."

After completing his studies, he came home to establish a meditation hall, call Zen'in-ji, and he lived there. His virtue in keeping the precepts attained perfection, while his wisdom was a constant source of light as clear as a mirror. He traveled far and wide, proclaiming Buddhist teaching to all beings. When he grew older, he remained at the meditation hall and lectured on the essentials of the scriptures he had brought back from China.

At the time of his death, he purified himself in the bath, changed his clothes, and seated himself facing west. Light filled the room, and he opened his eyes and asked his disciple Chicho, "Did you see the light?" Chicho replied, "Yes, I did." The Master Dosho asking him not to tell others of it. Very early the next morning a light emanated from the hall and moved round to illuminate to pine trees in the garden. Presently it flew away to the west. All of his disciples were struck with wonder, and it was at that very moment that the Most Venerable Master passed away seated calmly, facing west.

We are sure of his rebirth in the pure land of bliss. The note says: This member of the Fune family is extraordinary and not common, for he exemplified virtue, traveled far to seek for Buddhist scriptures, and ended his life in radiant light.

PRACTICING THE FORMULA OF THE PEACOCK KING AND THEREBY GAINING AN EXTRAORDINARY POWER TO BECOME A SAINT AND FLY TO HEAVEN IN THIS LIFE

E no ubasoku was of the Kamo-no-enokimi family, presently the Takakamo-no-asomi family. He came from the village of Chihara, Upper Kazuraki district, Yamato province. By nature he was endowed with wisdom; he excelled in learning-and attained ultimate knowledge. He lived with reverence and faith in the Three Treasures. His greatest desire was to fly on a five-colored cloud beyond the sky and play in the garden of eternity with the guests of the heavely palace, lying in the flowering garden and sucking the vital force out of the haze to nourish his nature.

Accordingly, in his late forties he went to live in a cave, wore clothing made of vines, drank the dewdrops on pine needles, bathed in pure spring water to rinse away the filth of the world of desire, and learned the formula of the Peacock to attain extraordinary power. Thus he could employ spirits and kami at his command at his command.

Once he summoned them all and ordered them, "Make a bridge between Kane-no-take and Kazuraki-no-take." They were not happy about this, and in the reign of the emporer residing at Fujiwara Palace, Hitokotonushi no Okami of Kazuraki-no-take was possessed and slandered him, saying, "E no ubasoku plans to usurp the throne." The emporer dispatched messengers to capture him, but they found it hard to take him due to his mysterious power, so they captured his mother instead. In order that his mother might be freed, he gave himself up.

He was exiled to the island of Izu. One time his body went floating on the sea as if he were walking on land. Again, his body perched on a mountain ten thousand feet high and looked like a huge phoenix in flight. In the daytime he stayed on the island in accord with the emporer's command, but at night he went to Fuji-no-take [Mt. Fuji] in Suruga to practice austerities. As he prayed for pardon from his severe punishment and for permission to return to the capital, he lay down on the blade of an assassin's sword and ascended Mt. Fuji. Three years passed in ascetic practice after he was exiled to the island. At the turn of the eighth year of the ox, the first year of the Taiho era, he was pardoned and approached the capital, finally becoming a saint and flying to heaven.

Dharma Master Dosho of our country received an imperial order to go to Great T'ang China in order to search out Buddhist teachings. On the request of five hundred tigers he went to Silla to lecture in the mountains on the Hoke-kyo. At that time there was a man among the tiger who raised a question in Japanese. The monk asked, "Who are you?" and the man answered, "E no ubasoku." The monk thought that the man was a Japanese sage and came down from his high seat to inquire about him, but he was gone.

Hitokotonushi no Okami was bound with a spell by E no gyoja, and he has not escaped even to this day. E no ubasoku did so many miraculous deeds that we cannot enumerate them all. Indeed we learn that Buddhist miraculous arts are comprehensive. Those who have faith will attain them without fail.

TAKING OTHERS' POSSESSIONS UNRIGHTEOUSLY, CAUSING EVIL, AND GAINING A PENALTY SHOWING AN EXTRAORDINARY EVENT

Kashiwade no omi Hirokuni was an assistant governor of Miyako district, Buzen province. In the reign of the emporer at Fujiwara Palace, on the fifteenth of the ninth month in the autumn of the second year of the snake, the second year of the Keiun era, Hirokuni passed away suddenly. On the fourth day after his death, about four o'clock in the afternoon, he was brought back to life and told the following tale:

> *"I went south to find my father standing and holding a hot copper pillar. He had thirty-seven nails in his body and was beaten with an iron stick, three hundred times in the morning, three hundred times in the*

afternoon, three hundred times in the evening, or, altogether, nine hundred times a day. I grieved at this and said, 'I never dreamed that you were suffering such punishment!' Then he spoke to me, saying, 'My son, probably you do not know why I am suffering. In order to support my family I killed living beings, pressed men to repay ten ryo on a loan of eight ryo of cotton, or lent rice and collected three times the amount. Also, I robbed others of their possessions, committed adultery with the wives of others, neglected filial piety and reverence to my elders, and used foul language to abuse those who were not slaves. Because of such offenses I have thirty-seven iron nails in my small body and receive nine hundred beatings daily with an iron stick. What pain! What suffering! When shall I be excused from my sin? When shall my body find rest? Please hurry to atone for my sins by making a Buddha-image and copying scriptures. Never forget this. When I visited you in hunger in the form of a big snake on the seventh of the seventh month and was about to enter the house, you picked up the sanke and threw it away. Again, when I went to your home in the form of a small red dog on the fifth of the fifth month, you call a big dog to chase me, and I left hungry and exhausted. However, when I house in the form of a cat on New Year's Day, I filled my stomach with the various offerings and was able to make up for three years' lack of food. Then, I lost my sense of social order and reason and became a dog eating and watering. I am sure to become a small red dog again.'

"If you make an offering of one quart of rice, you will gain a reward of thrity days food; if you make an offering of one set of clothes, you will gain a reward of one year's clothing. Those who have Buddhist scriptures recited will live in the eastern golden palace and be born in the heaven according to their wish; those who have Buddha-images made will be born in the Western Pure Land of Unlimited Life; those who set living beings free

will be reborn in the Northern Pure Land of Unlimited LIfe. Or, those who fast for a day will gain a reward of ten years' food.

"Shocked at the sight of so many instances of retribution, I came back to the big bridge. The guards watching the gate checked me and said, 'We cannot let you go out, since you have been in.' I was wandering around when the child appeared. The gatekeepers knelt to greet him. Then the child called me, led me to a side gate, and opened the door. When I was leaving, he said, 'Go quickly.' I asked him, 'Whose child are you?' He answered, 'If you want to know who I am, I am the Kanzeon-gyo which you copied in your childhood.' He was gone, whereupon I looked around to find myself in this world again."

As Hirokuni visited the land of the dead and saw the karmic retribution of good and evil, he recorded it for circulation. Who can fail to believe in the law of karmic retribution, as expounded widely in the Mahayana scriptures? This is what the scripture means when it says, "Honeydew in the present will be an iron ball in the future." Hirokune made Buddha images, copied scriptures, and made offerings to the Three Treasures to repay his father's love and atone for his sin, thereafter turning evil into righteousness.

GAINING AN IMMEDIATE REWARD FOR FAITH IN THE THREE TREASURES, REVERENCE TO MONKS, AND HAVING SCRIPTURES RECITED

In the ninth month of the fourth year of the hare, the fourth year of the Jinkai era, Emporer Shomu went hunting with his officers in the mountain at Yamamura in Sou upper district. A deer ran into a farmer's house in the village of Hosome, and the family killed and ate it without knowing whose it was. Later, when the emporer heard this, he sent messengers to take them prisoner. More than ten men and women met with this misfortune, and they shuddered in fear without any recourse. Their only thought was that nothing but the divine power of the Three Treasures would save them from their sad plight. As they heard that the Sixteen-foot Buddha of Daian-ji would respond to the people's prayers, they sent a man to visit the temple and have scriptures recited. They made an appeal to the monks, saying, "When we are led to court, please open the southern gate of the temple so that we may pay homage to the Buddha. Also we beg you to ring the bell when we are taken to court so that the sound of the bell may follow us."

According to their wishes, the monks rang the bell, recited scriptures, and opened the gate so that people might worship. The latter were sent to court by the messengers and confined in a guardroom. Just then a prince was born, and the emporer granted a general amnesty to criminals and did not punish them. Instead, he gave alms to the people, and their happiness and joy could not be measured.

We learn that this is due to the influence of the Sixteen-foot Buddha and the merit of reciting scriptures.

TAKING BACK SILK ROBES ONCE STOLEN OWING TO THE PETITION TO BODHISATTVA MYOKEN

Once there was a house in front of the Kisakibe-dera in Ate district, Kii province. As ten silk robes were stolen from the owners, they prayered devotedly through Bodhisattva Myoken in the temple. The stolen silk robes were sold to a merchant in Kii. Hardly a week passed before a gale hit, and the robes were whisked south on the back of a deer to the original owners' garden; the deer then disappeared in the heavens. The merchant who had brought them, hearing that they were stolen goods, did not ask for them back but kept quiet.

A NUN WHO PAINTED A BUDDHA IMAGE OUT OF GRATITUDE FOR THE FOUR KINDS OF BLESSINGS AND GAINED A POWER TO SHOW AN EXTRAORDINARY SIGN

In a village of Yuge, Wakae district, Kawachi province, there lived a highly disciplined novice nun. Her name is unknown. She lived in a mountain temple at Heguri, and, organizing a devotees' association, painted a Buddha image with a picture of the six existences in order to give thanks for the four kinds of blessings. When completed, it was enshrined in the temple after the dedication ceremony.

Meanwhile she left the temple, going from place to place on errands. During that time the picture was stolen, and she looked for it in vain, crying pitifully. Still leading the devotees' organization, she wanted to free living beings, and the members went to Naniwa to visit the market. When they saw a basket in a tree, they heard various animals crying in the basket. They waited for the owner to return, for they thought there must be animals in the basket and they wanted to buy them and set them free. Meanwhile, the owner returned. When they said to him, "We heard some animals in your basket, and we have been waiting to buy them from you," the owner said, "No, there is nothing alive in it." The nun did not give up, however. She continued begging till the merchants around them said to the owner, "You should open the basket." The owner was frightened, and he ran away, leaving the basket. When they opened it, they discovered the stolen image. In joy and tears the devotees cried, "Since we lost this image, we have been longing for it day and night. Now, by chance, we have found it. How happy we are!" When the merchants heard this, they gathered around and praised the nun's perseverence.

Joyfully the nun and the others set living beings free, held memorial services, and reconsecrated the image in the original temple, where it remained an object of devotion for both clergy and laity. This is indeed a miraculous event.

THE DEATH PENALTY IN THIS LIFE OF AN EVIL SON WHO TRIED TO KILL HIS MOTHER OUT OF LOVE FOR HIS WIFE

Kishi no Omaro came from the village of Kamo, Tama district, Musashi province. Omaru's mother was Kusakabe no Matoji. In the reign of Emporer Shomu he was appointed a frontier soldier at Tsukushi by Otomo (his name is unknown) and had to spend three years there. His mother accompanied him and lived with him, while his wife stayed behind to take care of the house.

Omaro, out of love for his wife who had been left behind, thought up the wicked idea of killing his mother and returning home to his wife, claiming exemption from duty on the pretext of mourning. As his mother's mind was set on doing good, he said to her, "There will be a great meeting for a week's lecture on the Hoke-kyo in the eastern mountain. Shall we go to hear the teaching?

His mother, deceived, was eager to go, and, devotedly purifying herself in a hot bath, accompanied her son to the mountain. Then he looked at her fiercely, as though with the eyes of a bull, and said, "You, kneel down on the ground!" Gazing at his face, she said, "Why are you talking like that? Are you possessed by a fiend?" The son, however, drew a sword to kill her. Kneeling down in front of her son, she said to him, "We plant a tree in order to get its fruit and to take shelter in its shade. We bring up children in order to get their help and to depend on them. What on earth has driven you so crazy! I feel as though the tree I have been depending on has suddenly ceased to protect me from the rain." He would not listen to her, so she sorrowfully took off her clothes, put them in three piles, knelt down, and told him her last wish: "Will you wrap up these clothese for me? One pile goes to you, my eldest son, one to my second son, and one to my third son."

When the wicked son stepped forward to cut off his mother's head, the earth opened to swallow him. At that moment his mother grabbed her falling son by the hair and appealed to Heaven, wailing, "My child is possessed by some spirit and driven to such an evil deed. He is out of his mind. I beseech you to forgive his sin." In spite of all her efforts to pull him up by the hair, he fell down. The merciful mother brought his hair back home to hold funeral rites and put it in a box in front of a Buddha image, asking monks to chant scriptures. How great was the mother's compassion! So much that she loved an evil son and practiced good on his behalf. Endeed, we know that an unfilial sin is punished immediately and that an evil deed never goes without a penalty.

COPYING THE HOKE-KYO WITH UTMOST DEVOTION AND WITNESSING AN EXTRAORDINARY EVENT

In the reign of Emporer Shomu, there was a man who made a vow in Sagaraka district, Yamashiro province. His name is unknown. He copied the Hoke-kyo in order to repay the four kinds of blessing and sent his messengers to the four quarters in search of sandalwood to make a container for the scrolls of the scripture. Eventually he bought it in the capital of Nara for one hundred kan and asked a craftsman to measure and make a container. When he tried to put the scrolls in it, he found he could not do so because the chest was too short. He was terribly disappointed, for he did not see how he could acquire such materials again. Therefore he made a vow, held a service as directed in the scripture, invited monks to confess offenses for three weeks, and wailing, he pleaded, "Please let me find such wood again." After two weeks he tried to put the scrolls in the chest and found that it had stretched a little of its own accord though it was still a little shorter than the scrolls. The man tried harder to discipline himself and to repent, and, at the end of the third week, he could put the scrolls in the chest. Wondering whether the scrolls had become shorter or the chest larger, he compared them with the original and found they were the same length. Indeed, we know that this was a test of the vowers supreme faith and a sign of the miraculous power of the Mahayana scripture. There can be no doubt about it.

THE IMMEDIATE REWARD OF SALVAGING THE LIVES OF A CRAB AND A FROG AND SETTING THEM FREE

Okisome no omi Taime was the daughter of a nun name Honi, the presiding officer of the nunnery of Tomi in the capital of Nara. She was so devoted in her pursuit of the path of Buddha that she preseverved her chastity. She used to collect herbs every day and serve them to the Most Venerable Gyogi.

One day she went to the mountains to collect herbs and saw a large snake swallowing a big frog. She entreated the snake, "Please set the frog free for my sake." But the snake would not. She entreated again, saying, "I will become your wife if you do me the favor of letting the frog go." On hearing that, the large snake raised its head high to see her face and disgorged the frog. Whereupon she said to the snake, "Come to me in seven days."

On the appointed day, she hid herself in the house with all the openings closed. The snake came as expected and knocked on the wall with its tail. The next morning, terrified, she went to her master, who lived at the mountain temple of Ikoma. He said to her, "You cannot break your promise.

Only be strict in observing the precepts." Therefore, she affirmed her faith in the Three Treasures and her acceptance of the five precepts, and returned home.

On the way she met a strange old man with a big crab. She said, "Who are you, old man? Will you please set the crab free for me?" He answered, "I am Edori no Nimaro from Uhara district, Settsu province. At the age of seventy-eight I had neither sons to depend upon nor the means of making a living. In Naniwa I happended to find this crab. I cannot give it to you, for I have promised it to someone." She took off her robe, begging him to sell her the crab in exchange for her robe, be he would not listen. She then took off her skirt to add to its price, and he finally agreed to her offer. Thereupon, she brought the crab back home and invited the Most Venerable Gyogi to hold a service for it, setting it free with a prayer. Impressed with her deed, the master exclaimed, "How noble! How good!"

That evening the snake came back again, climbed to the roof, and dropped into the house by pulling off part of the thatched roof. The terrified girl heard something jumping and flapping around in her bed, and the next morning she fund a big crab and a large snake that had been chopped into pieces. Then she realized that the crab she had liberated had come to her rescue out of gratitude. This was also due to the virtue gained by keeping the precepts. Although she wanted to unravel the mystery and tried to identify the old man, she could not find him. It was evident he was an incarnation of Buddha. This is a miraculous event.

THE PENALTY OF A FATAL DISEASE FOR ABUSING A MONK AND COMMITTING A LUSTFUL DEED

In the reign of Emporer Shomu, nuns of Saya-dera in Kuwahara, Ito district, Kii province, vowed to hold a service and invited a monk of Yakushi-ji on the West Side of Nara,

Dharma Master Daie (popularly called Dharma Master Yosami, for his secular name was Yosami no muraji), to perform the rite of repentance devoted to the Eleven-headed-Kannon.

It happened that a wicked man lived in that village. His surname was Fumi no imiki (his popular name was Ueda no Saburo). He was evil by nature and had no faith in the Three Treasures. The wife of this wicked man was a daughter of Kamitsuke no kimi Ohashi. She observed the eight precepts for one day and one night, and went to the temple to participate in the rite of repentance in the congregation. When her husband came home, he could not find her. Having asked where she was, he heard his servant say, "She has gone for the rite of repentance." At this he became angry and immediately went to the temple to bring his wife back.

The officiating monk saw him and tried to enlighten him, preaching the Buddhist doctrine. However, he would not listen to the monk, saying, "None of your nonsense! You vulgar monk, you seduced my wife! Watch out or you'll get your head smashed!" His vile speach cannot be described in detail. He called his wife to go home with him, and on their return he violated her. Suddenly an ant bit his penis, and he died in acute pain. He brought on his own death, immediate retribution, since he was so evil minded as to insult the monk unreservedly and not to refrain from wicked lust. Even if you have a hundred tongues in your mouth and utter a thousand words, never speak ill of monks. Otherwise you will incur immediate penalties.

LUSTFUL LOVE FOR THE IMAGE OF KICHIJO-TENNYO WHICH RESPONDED WITH AN EXTRAORDINARY SIGN A TALE FROM THE NIHON RYOIKI OF THE MONK KYOKAI

Once he dreamed of lying with the female deity and the next morning discovered a stain on the skirt of the image.

Seeing this, he repented, saying, "I prayed to you to give me a woman like yourself, but what a sacrifice you made to give yourself to me." He was too ashamed to tell others of the event. One disciple, however, heard about it in secret. When he was scolded and expelled from the temple because of disrespect for his teacher, he spoke ill of his teacher and revealed the whole affair. Villagers went to the temple to verify the rumor, and they discovered the stain on the statue. The lay brother could not deceive them and described in detail what had happened.

Indeed, we know that deep faith never fails to gain a response. To this effect the Nehan-gyo says: "A lewd man feels desire even for a woman in a picture."

THE IMMEDIATE REWARD OF THE DESTITUTE PRINCESS' DEVOTION TO THE IMAGE OF KICHIJO-TENNYO

In the reign of Emporer Shomu, twenty-three members of the imperial family agreed to give banquets and provide entertainment by turn. There was a poor princess among them. She had no means to give a banquet when the rest of the group had already done so. Being ashamed of her poverty, the effect of her past deeds, she went to Hatori-do on the East Side of Nara to worship the image of Kichijo-tennyo. In tears she said, "As I planted the seed of poverty in my former existence, I reap the fruit now. I went to the baquets, and, after consuming the food of others, I have no means to invite them in return. I implore you to bring me a fortune." At that moment her child ran to her in haste and said, "A great amount of food has been sent from the former capital." She ran out and found her former wet nurse saying, "I heard you had received guests and brought you food." The food and drinks were incredibly delicious and fragrant. Nothing was missing. The metal tableware was carried by thirty men.

All the princes invited to the banquet came and were delighted. There was twice as much food as for the preceeding banquets, and she was praised as a rich princess. Each one said, "If she were poor, how could she prepare such an extravagant banquet? It is better than the one I made before." The songs and dances were as extraordinary as the heavenly music. Some gave away their robes, some their skirts, and others coins, silk, cloth, cotton, etc. The princess, in her joy, gave the robes to her wet nurse to wear, but later, when she went to temple to worship the sacred image, she found the statue wearing them. Filled with doubt, she went to inquire to her former wet nurse who answered, "I do not know anything about your banquet."

Now it was evident that the bodhisattva had helped the princess out of sympathy. She acquired a fortune and henceforth escaped poverty. This is an unusual event.

THE REWARD OF COPYING THE HOKE-KYO AND HOLDING A SERVICE FOR A MOTHER IN REVEALING THE CAUSE OF HER REBIRTH AS A COW

Takahashi no muraji Azumabito was a very wealthy man in the village of Hamishiro, Yamada district, Iga province. He copied the Hoke-kyo for his mother, making a vow, saying, "I want to invite a monk related to my vow by karma to hold a service for her salvation." When he finished preparing a place for the service on the following day, he called a servant and said, "The first monk you happen to meet I will make the officiating monk. Don't overlook any monk who seems to be able to perform esoteric rites and bring him to me."

The servant went first, in accord with his master's request, to the village of Mitani in the same district. There he found a mendicant lying in the road, drunk, with a bag for a begging bowl at his elbow. His name is not known. He was sleeping so soundly that some mischievious person had shaved his head and hung a rope around him like a surplice without waking him. Seeing him, the servant woke him with a greeting and asked him to visit his master.

On his arrival, the master greeted him with respect and faith and kept him inside the house for a day and a night, during which time he made a clerical robe in haste and offered it to the mendicant.

The mendicant asked, "Why have you treated me like this?" and the host replied, "I would like to ask you to expound the Hoke-kyo." Then the mendicant said, "I have no learning. I have simply stayed alive by reciting the Hannya dharani and begging food." The host, however, repeated his entreaty. The mendicant thought to himself that the best way for him was a secret escape. Knowing the mendicant intended to run away, the host had him watched.

That night, the mendicant had a dream. A red cow came to him, saying, "I am the mother of the master of the household. Among his cattle there is a red cow, whose calf of none other than I. Once in my former life, I stole property from my son, and now I am atoning for it in the form of a cow. I have confided this to you with respect and sincerity since you are going to preach on the Mahayana scripture for me tomorrow. If you feel any doubt about my story, please prepare a seat at the back of the hall where you will preach tomorrow. You will find me seated there."

Awakening from this startling dream, the mendicant was very curious. The next morning, he went up to the lecturer's seat, saying, "I am ignorant of Buddhist teachings. I came to take this seat in compliance with my host's entreaty. But I have one thing to tell you, which is a revelation that came to me in a dream." Then he told about the dream in detail. Whereupon the host stood up, prepared a seat, and called the cow, which took the seat and lay down. In sorrowful tears he said, "Indeed this is my mother! I had no idea! Now I will forgive her."

The cow heard his words and sighed. When the service ended, the cow died suddenly. All the congregation cried so bitterly that there were echos of weeping in the hall and garden. Nothing has ever been so miraculous as this. The son continued to accumulate merits for his mother. We know that this miraculous event took place as a consequence of the son's extreme faith born of his feeling for his mother, and the mendicant's merits accumulated from reciting the divine dharani.

THE IMMEDIATE PENALTY OF BEING GIVEN A TWISTED MOUTH AND DEATH FOR SPEAKING ILL OF THE MONK, DEVOTEE OF THE HOKE-KYO

In the Tenpyo era (729-749), there once lived a layman in Sagaraka district, Yamashiro province, who name is unknown. At Koma-dera in the same district there was a monk named Eijo who used to recite the Hoke-kyo all the time. It happened that the monk and the layman had been playing go for some time. Whenever the monk put down his stone, he said, "This is the Venerable Eijo's hand of go." He went on and on this way. Then, all of a sudden, the layman's mouth was distorted. In fear, he left the temple holding his chin with his hands. He had hardly gone any distance before he fell on his back and died immediately. Witnesses said, "Though he did not persecute a monk, mocking and mimicking him got him a twisted mouth and sudden death. What, then, must the penalty be if one vengefully persecutes a monk?"

The Hoke-kyo gives a passages to this effect: "A wise monk and a foolish monk cannot be discussed in the same breath. Similarly, a long-haired monk and a wise, unshaved laymen cannot be treated alike and served with the same dishes. If one dares to do so, he will swallow an iron ball which is heated on red-hot copper and charcoal, and fall into hell."

THE MOTHER WHO HAD A BAD DREAM, WITH THE UTMOST FAITH HAD A SCRIPTURE RECITED, AND SAVED HER DAUGHTER BY AN EXTRAORDINARY SIGN

In the village of Yamamura in Sou upper district, Yamato province, there lived an aged mother whose name is unknown. She had a married daughter who bore two children. Her son-in-law was appointed provincial magistrate, and he took his family to his post. Several years passed.

Once the old mother, who had stayed in the home village to take care of the household, received an omen in a dream concerning her daughter. Surprised and fearful, she wanted to have a scripture recited for her daughter, but she was too poor to ask a monk to do it. As her mind was never free of worry for her daughter, she finally thought of taking off her robe and washing it to offer it to the monk for his service. Then another omen appeared in a dream. In even greater fear she took off her skirt, cleaned it, and, as she had done before, gave it as an offering to the monk for reciting a scripture.

Meanwhile her daughter was living in the official residence for a provincial magistrate at her husband's post. It happened that her children were playing in the court, while she herself was inside the back quarters. The two children saw seven monks seated on the roof reciting a scripture. They called to their mother, saying, "Mother, seven monks are chanting a scripture on the roof. Hurry! Come and see them!" The chanting sounded like bees humming together. Wondering at this, the mother had scarcely come out of the rear building when its wall collapsed. All of a sudden, the seven the monks disappeared. Greatly terrified and marveling at this accident, she thought to herself that heaven and earth had saved her from being crushed. Later, however, she heard from her mother who had sent a messenger to tell her about the evil omens and the subsequent services for the recitation of scriptures. She was so impressed with her mother's report that she professed faith in the Three Treasures with the greatest awe.

Thus we know that the whole sequence of events was generated by the power of reciting scriptures and the determination of the Three Treasures to protect us.

UNDERSTANDING KISHIMO-JIN AND OTHER CHILD-GIVING DEITIES

Kishimojin's Vow in The Lotus Sutra

Thereupon there were female rakshasas, the first named Lamba, the second named Vilamba, the third named Crooked Teeth, the fourth named Flowery Teeth, the fifth named Black Teeth, the sixth named Many Tresses, the seventh named Insatiable, the eighth named Necklace Holder, the ninth named Kunti, the tenth named Spirit Snatcher. These ten female rakshasas, together with the Mother of Demon Sons [Kishimojin] and her children and followers, all went to the Buddha and with one voice said to the Buddha: "World Honored One! We, too, would protect those who read and recite, receive and keep the Law-Flower Sutra, and rid them of corroding care. If any spy for the shortcomings of these teachers of the Law, we will prevent their obtaining any chance." Whereupon in the presence of the Buddha they delivered the following spell:

"Iti me, iti me, iti me, iti me, iti me; ni me, ni me, ni me, ni me, ni me; ruhe, ruhe, ruhe, ruhe, [ruhe]; stuhe,

stuhe, stuhe, stuhe, stuhe [svaha].

"Let troubles come on our heads, rather than on the teachers of the Law; neither yakshas, nor hungry ghosts...; nor fevers, whether for a single day, or quotidian, or tertian, or quartan, or weekly, or unremitting fevers; whether in male form, or female form, or form of youth, or form of a maiden, even in dreams shall ever cause distress. Whereupon before the Buddha they spoke thus in verse:

After these female rakshasas had uttered this stanza, they addressed the Buddha, saying: "World-honoured One! We ourselves will also protect those who receive and keep, read and recite, and practice this sutra, and give them ease of mind, freedom from corroding care and from all poisons."

The Buddha addressed the rakshasa women: "Good, good! Even if you are only able to protect those who receive and keep the name of the Law-Flower, your happiness will be beyond calculation; how much more if you protect those who perfectly receive, keep, and pay homage to the sutra! You and your followers should protect such teachers of the Law as these."

Historical Evolution of Kishimojin

A feminine form of Avalokitesvara, who facilitates childbirth and protects children, also exists. In Japan, this is a popular aspect of Juntei Kannon Bosatsu. She is Hariti, but a gentle 'Buddhicized' form of this 'mother of 'demons', She is often represented seated on a chair, clothed in the Chinese manner and holding child in her arms. Some popular images show her nursing a baby.

Owing to this aspect, she was venerated as a representation of the Christian Virgin Mary during the persecutions against Japanese converts to Christianity which took place in the Edo period, chiefly in the seventeenth and eighteenth centuries. In fact, Japanese Christians may have created this form of Avalokitesvara offering the breast, since it is not of buddhist origin. It is beleived that this form was developed late by popular Buddhism to supplant the Shinto deity (kami) of easy childbirth, Koyasu-sama or Koyasu-gami, just as in China the effigies of Guanyin shown with a child on the knees are probably merely popular Buddhist transpositions of Taoist 'child-giving' deities like Tianxin Songzi or Zhangxian.

In China, Tonkin and Japan, she is venerated in a group of 20 deities, among whom she hold a secondary place. In Japan, the Shinto sanctuaries dedicated to Koyasu-sama are actually dedicated to the mythical princess of Konohana Sakkuya Hime, goddess of Mount Fuji and of cherry trees in bloom, since legend claims that she gave birth to a son while her house was devoured by flames.

This may be an allusion to the creation of the lakes during an eruption of Mount Fuji. Koyasu-sama was mainly venerated in the provinces of Kanto (environs of Tokyo) and Chiba, where the women had the habit of asking her for healthy milk after childbirth in exchange for rice offerings.

Tradition relates that a statue of Koyasu Kannon was made in the eighth century in the image of the Empress Komyo (or Komei, 701-760), widow of the Emporer Shomu and mother of the Empress Koken, who became a nun in 1749. Undoubtedly, this feminine aspect of Avalokitesvara, the symbol of abnegation and love, contributed greatly to the spread of her cult in Japan. However, it was only from the fourteenth century, perhaps under the influence of the Nichiren sect, that people worshipped her statue as 'giver of children'. Some statues of Ksitigarbha are worshipped in the same way in Japan: they differ in no way from the normal images representing this Bodhisattva, except that she is named Koyasu Jizo Bosatsu, due to the powers attributed to her.

In Tibet, where her worship appears to date from early times, she is represented holding a child to her breast and a mongoose (nakula). She is also a 'dispenser of riches'. Her image appears to have been created in Gandhara, where she is shown as a Bodhisattva, but with visible fangs. She was also represented in Ajanta, in cave number 2, seated in Rajalilasana, above a frieze composed of many naked children. Some representations of her are also found in Java (e.g. at Chandi Mendut) and in central Asia. Her effigy is often accompanied by that of a Yaksa, Pancika, reputed to be the father of her children and a general in the army of Vaisravana.

3

Pre-eminent Women Disciples of the Buddha

MAHA PAJAPATI GOTAMI, FOUNDER OF THE ORDER OF NUNS

Pajapati Gotami was the Buddha's foster mother as well as his maternal aunt. King Suddodhana married both sisters Maya and younger sister Gotami. When queen Maha Maya died on the 7th day of the birth of Prince Siddattha her younger sister from that day became the queen and foster mother of the prince.

She felt miserably and lonely when Prince Siddhartha, Rahula his son and her own son Nanda renounced the worldly life for the higher life by entering the Noble Order. King Suddhodana also had passed away on attaining Arahatship. Ordination was now foremost in her mind.

She approached the Buddha on his visit to Kapilavathu and asked for the boon of forming the Order of the Nuns. But three times the Buddha turned down the request. She was dejected and returned home. Soon 500 maidens gathered round her. They too, felt the urge either through bereavement or following their beloved kith and kin to seek ordination.

So she determined to make amends. She shaved her hair and donned the yellow robe. Her 500 followers followed her example: Kapilavastu was separated from Jetavana monastery by a distance of 357 miles.

She covered the distance with her followers by foot although various chieftains and lords placed chariots at their disposal. The dusty roads in those days were quite unlike the roads of the present day. There were no pavements or sealed surfaces.

The gentle feet of Maha Pajapati Gotami were unused to such rough conditions. At the end of the journey they were thoroughly exhausted and travel-worn. The march caused a great stir in the district through which they passed. Such a walk attracted attention and soon the crowds lined the route. She felt that in the circumstances it was not fitting that she should court a refusal by the Buddha.

So she and her 500 companions lingered at the entrance of Jetavana monastery when to their great good fortune Venerable Ananda appeared. He was amazed to see his aunt in such a sorry state. He inquired whether any calamity had befallen the royal house of the Sakyans or whether there was a revolt. She assured him there was nothing of the kind but told him the purpose of her mission. Venerable Ananda was eminently fit to play the role of a mediator. Again and again Venerable Ananda entreated the Lord but only to be refused.

Finally, Venerable Ananda asked whether it was not possible for a woman to attain the bliss of sainthood. The Buddha responded by saying that a woman could attain as well as a man and then consented to the establishment of the Order for Nuns, but only on eight conditions.

These were the 8 conditions:

1. A Bhikkuni even if she was in the Order for 100 years must respect a Bhikkhu even of a day's standing.

2. A Bhikkuni should reside within 6 hours of travelling distance to and from the monastery where Bhikkhus reside for advice.
3. On Observance days a Bhikkhuni should consult the Bhikkhus.
4. A Bhikkhuni should spend the Vassa (rains retreat) under the orders of both Bhikhus and Bhikkhunis.
5. A Bhikkhuni should ply her life by both the orders.
6. A Bhikkhuni should on two years obtain the higher ordination (Upasampatha) by both Orders.
7. A Bhikkhuni cannot scold a Bhikkhu.
8. A Bhikkhuni cannot advise a Bhikkhu rather it should be the other way about.

When Venerable Ananda broached the news to Maha Pajapati Gotami she was glad. She wholeheartedly accepted the conditions laid down by the Buddha. She was true to her destiny, as not long afterwards she became an Arahant. So likewise did her companions on listening to the discourse called the Nandakovada Sutta by the Buddha. The King of Lichchavis built a residence for her and her followers at Vesali.

One day the Buddha accompanied by eighty Maha Arahants and a huge concourse of Bhikkhus visited Pinnacle Hall in the city of Vesali.

At such a sight Venerable Maha Pajapati Gotami was exceedingly glad. The disciples were fully worthy of the Lord as he was of them. She saw that Anna Kondanna, Sariputta, Mogallana, Khema, Uppalawanna, Nanda, Rahula and his mother Yasodhara (Bimba Devi) were to predecease the Lord. She was determined not to tarry but that she should be the first to go. Although she was 120 years old yet signs of old age were not visible. Her hair and teeth resemble those of a girl of 16 years. At the moment of her resolution of obtaining Parinibbana the earth trembled and quaked. The thunder in-the sky rent the air. Her companion's likewise sought release.

She and her companions proceeded to meet the Lord. Compliments were exchanged. Although from the 7th day the prince was reared by her the Buddha amply repaid the debt due to her by her ordination. She gave a graphic picture of the infancy of Prince Siddhartha. How she has fed and bathed the prince.

In the meantime people from far and near flocked to the scene as the news spread. Diverse deities came. Visva Kamma deity who by his psychic power came to the rescue to provide much needed accommodation.

The Buddha requested Venerable Maha Pajapati Gotami to clear doubts about her sainthood. Then she paid tribute by performing many miraculous acts and all present including the Maha Arahants marvelled.

She and her companions underwent the great release - Parinirvana. At last the cremation came to pass. The Lichchavi Princes brought sandalwood for the funeral pyre and the caskets containing the remains were made ready. The whole sky was overcast with the heavenly host during the day. The stars and the moon shone brilliantly overhead as night followed. People laid carpets and the deities held a canopy overhead.

It was a unique ceremony the Buddha and the Maha Arahants graced, so the pyre was lit and only the relics of Venerable Maha Pajapati Gotami remained like pearls and those of others vanished from the scene. These relics were placed in the Buddha's bowl and given to him. The Buddha extolled the virtues of this great Arahant. He himself had ordained her and been her teacher and this was said to dispel any doubts.

The Buddha had a stupa built by the Lichavi Prince and the relics enshrined and the Buddha Himself joined the funeral procession. This was a unique honour paid by the Tathagata.

The Buddha addressing the Monks and laity declared that Venerable Maha Pajapati Gotami was foremost in attainments among the female Maha Arahants of the Noble Order.

THE NUN, KHEMA

In the Dispensation of Gautama Buddha Khema was born in a princely family at Sagala by the name of Khema. The colour of her complexion was that of gold. She was exceptionally beautiful. She married King Bimbisara of Kosala who was an enthusiastic supporter of the Buddha. She was reluctant however, to visit the Buddha for fear that the Blessed One would moralise on the fleeing nature of beauty.

Every time she visited the monastery she dodged meeting the Buddha. One day the king got his men to take her to the Buddha without her suspecting a meeting had been arranged. On her arrival, the Buddha created a phantom of unsurpassing beauty to attend on Him. The beauty of the phantom overwhelmed Khema. While she was thus engaged she felt that beauty could only beguile. The Buddha made the figure to go through youth, middle age, and old age and thereafter to extreme old age devoid of everything worthwhile. Beauty thus gave way to hideousness. It was a graphic picture. Khema understood the meaning and felt what was in store for her: Anicca, Dukkha and Anatta in other words transiency, sorrow and not-self.

To a mind thus prepared the Buddha taught. The seeds fell on good ground. She entered the stream of sainthood (sotapanna). The Buddha illustrated His teaching by bringing before her mind the lesson of the spider and the web. As soon as a fly strikes a web, the spider by the motion thus generated takes it as a signal and attacks by devouring the fly. The spider became wedded to the web. In like manner human beings are wedded to passion and lust. Her mind 'insighted' into this and she became an Arahant. She asked permission from the king for her ordination. The king, himself an aspiring saint, readily consented. One day the god Mara in the guise of a young man tempted Khema, and was rebuffed. His discomfiture was complete and he fled. One night Khema thought of visiting the Buddha. But the Buddha was with Sakka king of the gods. Rather than disturb the Buddha, Khema wheeled round in the air and disappeared.

Sakka on seeing the vision was soon enlightened of the matter by the Buddha.

The Buddha addressing the monks and the laity, declared that Khema of his female disciples was the most eminent for Wisdom.

"Fair maid lost in thy beauty;

Was rescued by the Great Sage.

Thy mind was keen as razor's edge;

Thou heard the call of Duty".

SUBHA - THE ENLIGHTENED NUN

Because she had observed her precepts well as a good devotee of a former Buddha, Subha was born as the beautiful daughter of a prosperous goldsmith during the dispensation of Lord Gotama Buddha. Since her birth brought good luck to the household, her proud father named her Subha, which means "Lucky." He often thought, "This daughter of mine promises to be a perfect beauty. She reminds me of the superb royal jewellery I make!"

By the time Subha reached her sixteenth year, her father had become a rich man, receiving commissions from many rich clients. As his trade prospered, he had many goldsmiths working under him. Subha often wore the beautiful necklaces, coronets, and other ornaments he crafted for queens and princesses, parading and showing off their beauty. The parents and neighbors admired good-natured Subha, who appeared even more beautiful wearing delicate, refined ornaments. As Subha was kind, her home was a happy place, where friends and relations assembled in harmony.

Subha's neighbors often talked of a royal prince who had left his palace to lead an ascetic life. They said that the noble Sage had become a great saint, with many disciples. One day when the people of Rajgriha expected the noble sage's arrival, Subhas' father declared that day a holiday for his workmen and the maid Subha went with her parents and friends to witness the great sage's arrival. When the populace, led by King Bimbisara, heard the Lord Buddha's teachings, they were filled with joy. By evening the king, his retinue, and all the citizens of the town had accepted Buddhism as their faith. Very soon monasteries were offered to the Buddha, where some of the monks stayed, while others set forth to preach the doctrine.

Soon Buddhism was the accepted religion of the country. Many young men and women joined the Order of monks and nuns. Subha accompanied her parents to the teaching site and listened happily to the discourses. She saw the yellow-robed nuns and spoke with them. Her family became good devotees who often visited the monastery. One day, as the Lord surveyed the audience with supernormal vision, he saw that the maid Subha was experiencing last birth in samsaric existence - that she would become a nun and gain enlightenment. As the Lord preached that day, Subha listened intently and, at the end of the discourse, she attained the stage of a Stream Entrant. Thereupon she pleaded with her parents to allow her to become a nun. The parents were reluctant to part with her since, as their only child, she was slated to inherit their wealth. So, because they loved her, they tried their best to change her mind. In the end, however, they relented and, in due course, she became a nun. Her parents and relations thought that Subha would soon leave the nunnery and return to them, since she was fond of wearing fine clothes and jewellery.

Meanwhile Subha received doctrinal instructions from the nuns and observed her precepts well.

She listened well when the nuns preached the Dharma and discussed doctrinal topics at length. She received instructions on meditation and meditated peacefully. Without her, the fond parents' home became a desolate place. Eventually, they talked over with friends and decided to visit the nunnery with the idea of coaxing Subha to return home. As they visited the nunnery, her mother began to weep, saying: "Dear daughter! Our home is a desolate place without you. Think of the lovely gold jewellery made specially for you by your father! These ornaments decorated your neck, ears, and arms! Once you loved to wear them! Now we have no daughter to inherit them! Dear daughter, we are rich with much wealth and many servants! Return and be the owner of all our wealth!" Her relations and friends made the same appeal while the mother cried.

Subha, determined to stop further appeals, tried to convince them that their appeals were in vain. She advised them with these words:

Listen well, my mother and relations.

Attired nicely as befitted a youth,

I listened to the teachings of the Lord.

In a wholesome state of mind,

I then realised the Truth.
So I left my parents who loved me,
My devoted friends and relations all,
All luxuries of a comfortable life,
Considerable wealth, lands and fields.
Craving for worldly comforts,
Does not suit my life now.
I left my homey comforts.
I shall not go there again,
I prefer a life of solitude,
Devoid of all craving.
Those fallen into the abyss of desire,
Often face disappointments,
Loss of their wealth,
Bodily hurt and even worse disasters.
Dear relations, listen to me.
Why do you try to tempt me
With all the troubles that I have left behind?
Dear friends, please realise that I am a homeless nun,
Who discerns no value in wealth!
My head is shaven;
I am clad in the robes of the Order.
Please realize my homeless mendicant state!
Living on whatever food others offer me,
Wearing robes that others offer me,
Living according to the precepts -
Such is the life of a nun.
Omniscient Lord Buddha,

As well as the noble Sangha,
Have shattered all bonds of desire
To attain the freedom of liberation.
They are free and happy!
Craving and desire are frightful enemies.
Like a devastating fire, they bring
All troublesome sorrows in their wake.
Like enemies, they chose to punish us.
Sensual pleasures are a terror,
Poisoning the minds of people.
Like a poisoned dart, they pierce the pure mind,
Misleading people to danger and sin.
Pleasures of the senses are frightful,
Like a snake's head about to sting.
Those ignorant people,
Who unable to cross the mire of desire,
Wallow in the pleasures of the senses.
They see no end in birth and death,
In the vast sea of existence.
Thus craving brings forth,
Rebirth in sorrowful conditions.
Their feed are as if bound
Forever in the ocean of samsaric existence.
Greed and desire create foes,
Enticing followers to danger.
Repenting their folly,
They face endless sorrows.
Partaking of sugar-coated poisoned food,

They are happy, singing at first.
As the poison works, it brings much torment.
Suffering and disaster follow in its wake.
Therefore, dear friends and relations,
For these reasons, I do not accept
Your ideas of happiness dependent on wealth.
I have found happiness in being a nun.
Never will I accept home life again!
Even as the Noble Ones,
Who followed the Noble Eightfold Path,
Were able to cross the fearful ocean of samsara,
I shall certainly follow their steps,
To gain the bliss of nibbana.

The friends and relations who listened never tempted her again. Most of them realised the truth of her words, and were happy when they listened to her.

Meditating on peace, Subha was able to attain her goal of attaining full liberation on the eighth day after her ordination. One day, as the enlightened nun was enjoying the bliss of meditation, Lord Buddha pointed her out to the nuns who came to worship him, saying: "Nuns! Look at the nun Subha! She has been well-trained by Theri Uppalavanna. Full of faith, she has maintained mindfulness and restrained her senses. By earnest endeavour, she has gained deliverance from the bonds. Her practice has culminated in the full attainment of Arahantship. She has reached the Three Higher Knowledges. It is only eight days since she received ordination. She is indeed a credit to the Order of Nuns!" When Sakra, the king of the gods, overheard the Lord's words, he came with his retinue of heavenly beings and worshipped the enlightened nun Subha.

4

Women in Theravada Buddhism

Buddhism has, throughout its history, slowly moved east, from India through China, Burma, Thailand, Vietnam, Korea, Japan. Most recently, it has begun its jump across the ocean to the United States. With each move, the expression of Buddhism has changed to suit the culture of the people. Buddhism has not yet been in the United States (or any other Western country) long enough to develop into a clear new form, suitable for Western culture. There are many aspects of traditional Buddhism which need slight adaptation in order to be accepted within the complex structures of Western society.

One of the areas of traditional Buddhism which modern Western Buddhists find the most problematic is the area of gender. In most Asian Buddhist traditions, the leaders and teachers are all male, while females are given less prestigious roles.

Western Buddhists tend to come from highly educated and socially liberal backgrounds, which means that they tend to feel that men and women are equal and should be given equal opportunities in all endeavors. This difference of opinion between Western and Asian Buddhists causes a certain amount of tension. As a female Western Buddhist,

I am naturally extremely interested in this issue. While admittedly it may have little bearing upon men's practice on Buddhism, it has the potential to have an enormous effect upon my practice of Buddhism. I decided to use the opportunity this paper presented me to examine the role of women in Theravada Buddhism. Theravada is the oldest and most traditional of the various sects of Buddhism being imported to the United States. In order to understand the current situation, it is necessary to understand the historical setting. Therefore, I thought I would start by examining the role of women in early Buddhism, and trace the historical role of women in Theravada Buddhism through to the present.

What, then, was the role of women at the time of the Buddha? The historical Buddha lived in northern India at approximately 500 BCE. Women seem to have held an extremely subordinate place in the society in which he lived. They spent their lives serving. A typical woman spent her youth serving and obeying her parents, her middle years serving and obeying her husband and his parents, and her old age serving and obeying her grown children. Women usually had to marry the husband chosen for them by their parents, although occasionally young women would be given the choice of several suitors. The literature also mentions occasional elopements, without the permission of parents. However, for the most part, daughters could be married off at the discretion of their fathers.

Once married, women were supposed to obey their husband and his parents. Wives cooked, cleaned, bore and raised children, and looked after the servants. Women ate only what was left after the men had finished eating. If a husband was displeased with his wife, he could beat her or throw her out of the house. Divorce could be initiated by the husband, but not the wife. Women were supposed to bear children for their husbands. If no children were forthcoming, the husband would often take another wife. Adulterous wives were punished with death, while adulterous husbands were not punished at all. There were instances in which husbands would give their wives away to other men. Women were lowered nearly to the point of being mere chattel.

There were, of course, some women who were courtesans or prostitutes. Some women chose this life for themselves. Others had less choice. It is recorded that in Vaisali, there was a law forbidding a perfect woman to marry, and demanding that she be made available for the pleasures of the people. There were both advantages and disadvantages to the life of a courtesan. Courtesans often learned to play music and to dance. They were relatively independent, and could earn their own living. They had an accepted place in society. However, their lives were unsafe. As they had no one protecting them, they easily fell victim to robbers and murderers.

Many women were lower-class servants or slaves. These women had to follow all of the orders of their masters. Most of them worked hard all day, everyday. They could not marry without the permission of their masters. The slave women did not have the right to refuse the sexual advances of their masters. If the masters chose, they could beat the slave women to death. There are instances recorded in which slave women were beaten so regularly and heartlessly by their masters that they committed suicide.

In all their roles, women were less powerful than were men. As Janice Willis says,

> *"They were helpmates at best and burdens at worst, but always they were viewed as being inferior, second class citizens."*

Women seldom were allowed to make their own decisions. They were told what to do by men and spent their lives in service to others. This, then, is the society in which the Buddha grew up and taught. Into this culture, the Buddha made what would have then been a radical statement on the potential of women. When asked by Ananda (his closest disciple) the Buddha said that women are capable of becoming arhats. If women follow the path of renunciation, they can become completely enlightened, just as men can. Elsewhere in the scriptures, the Buddha elaborates on this idea, while using the imagery of a chariot to explain the Buddhist path:

> *" 'Straight' is the name that Road is called, and 'Free From Fear' the Quarter whither thou art bound. Thy Chariot is the 'Silent Runner' named, With Wheels of Righteous Effort fitted well. Conscience the Leaning-board; the Drapery Is Heedfulness; the Driver is the Dharma, I say, and Right Views, they that run before. And be it woman, or be it man for whom Such a chariot doth wait, by that same car into Nirvana's presence shall they come." 2*

Thus we find the Buddha teaching that not only can women reach the same levels of enlightenment as can men, but women also follow the same path to get there. The Buddha does not say that there are no differences between men and women. However, in these statements, he seems to feel that any differences between men and women are unimportant in the pursuit liberation.

The Buddha acted upon his conviction that women and men could pursue liberation in the same way. He established both an order of bhikkhus (monks) and an order of bhikkhunis (nuns). The two orders practiced in the same way and most of the rules governing them were identical. The Buddha also preached to both men and women. He was willing to teach anyone who was willing to learn. He put himself out of his way to bring both women and men to a deeper understanding. His belief that women could become arhats in the same way men could was validated by the enlightenment of many of his female followers.

However, the portrait of the Buddha painted by the Pali canon does not always validate the efforts of women to practice a life of renunciation. In an oft quoted passage, the Buddha is entreated by his step-mother to ordain an order of nuns. He warns her to be wary of the idea. She and a large group of women who want to be nuns dress as nuns, shave their heads, and walk barefoot to Vesali, where the Buddha had gone. They arrive at the Buddha's door crying, with swollen feet. Ananda is moved by their determination and sincerity, and pleads their case with the Buddha. The Buddha at first refuses to ordain the women, although he admits that women who live the monastic life can attain arhatship. Eventually, Ananda changes the Buddha's mind, and the women are ordained as nuns. However, the Buddha insists that they take upon themselves eight rules which place the nuns in a position decidedly subordinate to the monks. He also warns that his teachings, which would have lasted a thousand years, will only last five hundred years because of the ordination of the nuns.

Why does the Buddha, who is usually willing to bend over backwards to promote the growth and enlightenment of every person, suddenly so hesitant and gloomy when confronted with the opportunity to institutionalize a path towards enlightenment for women?

Some recent commentators have argued that this incident never really happened, but was invented later in order to justify changes to the status of the bhikkhunis which were made to bring the practice of institutional Buddhism more in line with societally accepted norms. In other words, the Buddha thought of men and women as equal, and made the bhikkhus and bhikkhunis equal. After his death, the society could not deal with the existence of a group of women which were acknowledged to be equal with or superior to most men. Monastic Buddhism had to be acceptable to lay society, because the monastics were completely supported by the lay people. Therefore, various rules were made to lower the status of the bhikkhunis, and this story was invented to justify the change. This explanation of the story of the Buddha's reluctance is possibly correct. The scriptures were not written down until four hundred years after the Buddha's death, which gave plenty of time for small changes to creep into the stories.

Other modern commentators feel that the story is an accurate representation of what actually happened. These people feel that the Buddha himself must have been aware of the problems society would have in accepting an independent order of nuns. He made the rules about the bhikkhunis' subordinance to the bhikkhus especially to mitigate action against the bhikkhunis. These rules call for gestures of submission on the part of the bhikkhunis, but in no way diminish the bhikkhunis' ability to meditate and follow the path towards enlightenment. The Buddha may have seen this as the best way to preserve women's ability to work towards enlightenment within the confines of their society.

These commentators generally explain the Buddha's statement about the amount of time his teaching would survive by saying that the Buddha felt that it was as valuable to reach twice as many people (both men and women) for half the length of time (five hundred rather than one thousand). It is possible that the Buddha thought his teaching would end sooner if women were ordained because he thought that society simply wouldn't accept a teaching which allowed that much freedom for women.

All commentators agree that what was new and important about Buddha's teachings about women was that women could attain arhatship and that women could do so by following basically the same path as men. Certain limitations were made on the social equality of bhikkhus and bhikkhunis, and these limitations were probably made in order to increase societal acceptance of the monastic orders.

In any case, Buddha opened the doors for women's entrance to monastic life. Women flocked by the thousand to join the order of bhikkhunis. Women joined for all sorts of reasons. Many women joined simply because the Buddha's teachings made sense to them, and aroused in them a desire for liberation. Other women, though this first reason was true for them, had other reasons as well. Some become bhikkhunis because their husbands or other relatives were becoming bhikkhus. Others became bhikkhunis when they were widowed, or when their other relatives died. Some very poor women joined because the order would provide them with some measure of security. Courtesans who were disgusted with their lives of sex left to become bhikkhunis. Some young women chose the renunciate's life as preferable to marriage.

Women had more freedom and independence within the order of bhikkhunis than anywhere else in society. Bhikkhunis were not anyone's slave or servant. For the most part, they ran their own community and made their own decisions. They seldom had to take orders from any one and did not have look after anyone's physical needs. They were specifically forbidden to do household chores. They had only to work for liberation from samsara. Once they, themselves, were liberated, then they often taught other women.

And many women became liberated, becoming arhats. There are dozens of instances of female arhats in the Pali canon. There must have been many more who were not recorded. These women were often accomplished speakers who led many other women to liberation. Some of their words are recorded in the Pali canon. These snippets show the female arhats' delight and self-confidence in their freedom from traditional women's positions. Soma, a bhikkhuni and contemporary of the Buddha, was taunted thus:

> *"That vantage point the sages may attain Is hard to win. With her two-fingered consciousness, That place no woman is competent to gain."*
>
> *" Soma replied: What should the women's nature signify When consciousness is taut and firmly set, When knowledge rolleth ever on, when she by insight rightly comprehends the Dharma?"*

Soma clearly felt that her femininity was no obstacle to her enlightenment. She acted with self-confidence and poise. Her position was completely in accord with the Buddha's teaching of anatman, or no-self. This teaching states that people have no fixed or permanent nature. All human attributes are in a constant state of change, and are not inherently real. If we see something that looks real, like "women's nature," we simply need to transcend this illusory attribute.

The greatest source of women's voices in the Pali canon is in the Therigatha--the enlightenment songs of the early bhikkhunis. Although the Therigatha was probably edited by monks, it still allows us a glimpse of the early bhikkhunis' delight at their freedom. For example, a nun named Mutta wrote:

> *"Free I am free I am free from the three crooked things: mortar, pestle, and my crooked husband. I am free from birth and death and all that dragged me back".*

Bhikkhunis were not the only women who were important in the early years of Buddhism. Lay women were also important in the early vitality of the sect. Many women who were converted to Buddhism did not join the order of bhikkhunis. Quite a number of these women gained some level of enlightenment, and a few even became arhats. Perhaps more important to the young movement, however, was the financial support of wealthy lay women.

Wealthy women gave the monastic orders mansions, money with which to construct monasteries, material for robes, bowls, food, medicine, and so forth. Historical studies have found that during the first seven or eight centuries of Buddhism in India, Buddhism was patronized by wealthy queens. These women provided a large portion of the material wealth of the monasteries, as well as probably helping the political position of the Buddhists. Although we cannot definitively say that Buddhism would not have survived that period without the help of the queens, it is certain that Buddhism would not have prospered nearly as much as it did.

On a more mundane level, most of the daily giving of food to the bhikkhus and bhikkhunis was done by lay women, as they were the ones who traditionally prepared and served food. Thus, the daily life of the renunciates required interaction with the lay women. As the bhikkhus were supposed to be celibate, this constant interaction with lay women could cause quite a problem.

The lay women provided a temptation and a target for lust. In defense against their own lustful tendencies, the bhikkhus developed a misogynistic philosophy. For example, in the Anguttara-Nikaya (vi, 5, III, 56), monks are warned:

> *"Monks, a woman, even when going along, will stop to ensnare the heart of a man; whether standing, sitting or lying down, laughing, talking or singing, weeping, stricken, or dying, a woman will stop to ensnare the heart of a man. Monks, if ever one would rightly say:*

> *"It is wholly a snare of Mara," verily, speaking rightly, one may say of womanhood: "It is wholly a snare of Mara."*

This point of view was given credence by the circumstances surrounding many monks' entrance to the order. Often, husbands abandoned their wives and children in order to become monks. As the women were left with little financial support and a greatly reduced status in society, they often tried to woo their husbands back. Although this tendency to present women as temptresses did have the positive effect of helping the monks resist the temptation to renounce the monastic life, it also had the negative effect of vilifying women. It placed the blame for monks' feelings of lust on the women instead of on the monks. These misogynistic ideas also provided support for reducing the freedoms allowed to bhikkhunis.

So what happened to the order of bhikkhunis in the centuries after the Buddha's death? The order flourished for several centuries. It is claimed that in the third century B.C.E., 96,000 bhikkhunis once gathered in Jambudipa. This is probably an exaggeration, but the order was clearly thriving.

In the same century, Mahinda and some other monks travelled from India to Sri Lanka to convert the inhabitants to Buddhism. He preached to many people, converting many. He started an order of bhikkhus there. Queen Anula and her maidens heard him and were impressed by his wisdom. They wanted to become bhikkhunis, but he told them that he could not ordain them. Traditionally, it takes ten bhikkhus to ordain a bhikkhu, and both ten bhikkhus and ten bhikkhunis to ordain a bhikkhuni. Mahinda sent for his sister, Sanghamitta, who was a bhikkhuni in India. She came, with eleven other bhikkhunis, and started the nuns' order in Sri Lanka. This happened in approximately 250 B.C.E.

The bhikkhunis in Sri Lanka propagated the faith and also seem to have worked as nurses. In the early fifth century C. E.,- Sri Lankan bhikkhunis went to China and established an order of nuns there. As the centuries progress, there is less and less mention of the bhikkhunis. By the third century C. E. there is almost no mention of bhikkhunis in India, although we know the order survived there in some form until at least the seventh century. There is similarly little mention of Sri Lankan bhikkhunis.

We do know that the bhikkhunis were declared wards of the king, and their monasteries were kept within the walled interiors of major cities, where they could (theoretically) be protected. The last certain reference to them is at the end of the tenth century. By then the order was not very numerous. The nuns were probably largely controlled by the edicts of the monarchy, and spent much of their time working as nurses and performing other social duties. It seems unlikely that they maintained much of their original spiritual autonomy and freedom to pursue enlightenment.

In the eleventh century, Sri Lanka was conquered by the Colas of southern India. The Colas destroyed all the monasteries and killed the monks and nuns. When the Colas were finally defeated in 1070, the new government worked to restore Buddhism. They managed to get some monks from Burma to come and restore the order of bhikkhus, but there were no surviving orders of Theravada nuns. (Buddhism had pretty much disappeared in India by this time.) Since ten nuns were needed to ordain a new nun, ordination of bhikkhunis stopped. Since that time, there has been no fully ordained order of Theravada bhikkhunis.

Thus, for the last millennium, female Theravada Buddhists have had to content themselves with lay life. The primary religious practice available to them has been support of the bhikkhus. While lay women's support has certainly been useful for the continuance of institutional Buddhism, it is questionable whether this support has been similarly useful in freeing women to attain nirvana.

Clearly, not all Sri Lankan women have been content to pursue nirvana only in the limited ways permitted by traditional lay life. By the end of the nineteenth century a group of women had appeared in Sri Lanka who had renounced the lay life and vowed to keep the ten precepts (the most basic of the monastic vows). These women are referred to as "Dasa-Sil-Maniyo," (DSM) or mothers of the ten precepts. As of 1984, there were approximately 2500 such women in Sri Lanka.

These women live very much as bhikkhunis used to. To most people's eyes they would appear to be bhikkhunis. They shave their heads and wear saffron colored robes, just as the bhikkhunis did. They spend much of their time teaching people about Buddhism, meditating, and participating in Buddhist ceremonies. However, both the DSM and the people of Sri Lanka insist that the DSM are not bhikkhunis, because they could not be properly ordained by ten bhikkhunis and ten bhikkhus, as was the custom.

Not being allowed proper ordination has made life difficult for the DSM. Traditionally, laity gain merit by donating to ordained monastics much more than they gain merit by donating to lay people. Therefore, the laity do not feel they have strong religious reason to help support the DSM. Consequently, the DSM are poverty stricken. According to one recent report,

> *"The majority have no proper dwellings, no means of subsistence, no provision for obtaining clothing and material for their robes, and . . . no opportunity is given them to improve their understanding of the religion."*

The government of Sri Lanka is making some attempt to rectify this unfortunate state of affairs. I do not know how much success this effort has had.

There is also a very small group of women in Sri Lanka who claim to be real bhikkhunis. They live in a cloister in the same complex as a a cloister of bhikkhus. The chief monk of the complex explains the claim that the women are bhikkhunis by pointing out that the traditional ordination was merely a custom, begun to encourage institutional stability. The Buddha only preached about the monastic life, and not about the details of ordination, so it is the monastic life which is important. What matters is that the monastic women properly understand the dharma and vow to follow the monastic rules. It is this that makes them bhikkhunis. This argument, however, is not accepted as valid by most Sri Lankans. This order of modern bhikkhunis does not seem likely to prosper. Thus, the two primary choices offered to female Buddhists in Sri Lanka are the life of a lay woman, supporting the bhikkhus, or the life of a marginalized quasi-monastic lay-nun.

And what of the West? How is Theravada Buddhism being incorporated into the lives of female Western followers? There are women in the United States who are living lives much like those of the DSM. These women dress like nuns and accept the ten precepts, but are not officially ordained. They often have difficulties similar to the DSM in Sri Lanka. The monastic women who live alone have difficulty supporting themselves and often have to resort to taking paid jobs just so they can eat and have a place to live. Doing paid work is against the traditional monastic rules, but these women have little other choice but to starve. They often have difficulty receiving religious instruction.

Other monastic women live in temples or meditation centers. These women are usually more financially secure and have regular religious instruction. However, they have to abase themselves before monks regularly. Western monastic women must let monks eat first, must sit in the back of the room during religious instruction, and must bow down before all monks, no matter what their level of religious attainment. Western women are not brought up to humble themselves before men, so these traditions tend to rankle enormously. There are a few women who are so involved with the meditation practice that they scarcely seem to notice the sexist social structure within which they practice. Other women are acutely aware of the sexism and try to ignore it so that they can reap the benefit of the actual practice.

These women tend to try to use the humbleness demanded of them as a practice, but often they cannot help but mind the fact that this humbleness is not required of male practitioners. Although the Buddha taught that the same path leads women and men to enlightenment, women and men are given somewhat different paths.

A number of women have split off from the traditional monastic paths. These women, after receiving extensive training in Theravada Buddhist meditation, have become independent teachers of meditation and the dharma. They continue to follow the basic Buddhist precepts, but disregard all traditional limitations put on women. They bow down only to people whom they feel are more advanced than they are, themselves. They live where they choose and wear what they choose. Some of them are married. They teach both men and women. They often teach traditional Theravada meditation, but they sometimes combine Theravada meditation with the practices of other sects of Buddhism, or even practices of completely different religions. They often explain the dharma in their own language, eschewing the traditional explanations in favor of language less foreign to typical lay Americans. From the perspective of traditional Theravada practice, these women are renegades, scarcely similar enough to most Theravadans to be worthy of the identification.

Yet I suspect that these women, revolutionary as they are, probably point the way to the future of American Buddhist practice. Their way is one of dissolving boundaries. They dissolve the boundaries between various Buddhist sects, between traditional Buddhist language and secular American language, between lay and monastic life, and between traditional male and female roles. Somehow, all this dissolving of boundaries strikes me as being quite true to the Buddha's original teachings. Although Theravada Buddhism as traditionally practiced may not survive in the melange that will probably become American Buddhism, I have a feeling that the most important pieces of the Theravada tradition will be preserved. At least, I hope so. I have high hopes for the ultimate outcome of the peculiar admixture of American independence and Buddhist liberation.

5

The Status of Women in Buddhism

Today, when the role of Women in Society is an issue of worldwide interest it is opportune that we should pause to look at it from a Buddhist perspective. In the recent past, a number of books have been written on the changing status of women in Hindu and Islamic societies, but with regard to women in Buddhism, ever since the distinguished Pali scholar, Miss I.B. Horner, wrote her book on Women under Primitive Buddhism, as far back as 1930, very little interest has been taken in the subject.

It seems, therefore, justified to raise again the question whether the position of women in Buddhist societies was better than that in non-Buddhist societies of Asia. We will look briefly into the position in Sri Lanka, Thailand, Burma and Tibet, at a time before the impact of the West was ever felt.

Hugh Boyd who came as an envoy to the Kandyan Court in 1782 writes,

> *The Cingalese women exhibit a striking contrast to those of all other Oriental Nations in some of the most prominent and distinctive features of their character. Instead of that lazy apathy, insipid modesty and sour austerity, which have characterized the sex throughout*

the Asiatick world; in every period of its history, in this island they possess that active sensibility, winning bashfulness and amicable ease, for which the women of modern Europe are peculiarly famed. The Cingalese women are not merely the slaves and mistresses, but in many respects the companions and friends of their husbands; for though the men be authorized by law to hold their daughters in tyrannical subjection, yet their sociable and placable dispositions, soften the rigor of their domestic policy. And polygamy being unknown and divorce permitted among the Cingalese, the men have none of that constitutional jealousy, which has given birth to the voluptuous and unmanly despotism that is practiced over the weaker sex in the most enlightened nations, and sanctioned by the various religions of Asia. The Cingalese neither keep their women in confinement nor impose on them any humiliating restraints.

The above quotation is just one selected from a series of comments which European observers have made on the women of Sri Lanka. Many of these European visitors to our shores came during the 17th, 18th and early 19th centuries.

There were among them, envoys, missionaries, administrators, soldiers, physicians and ship-wrecked mariners. They had first-hand knowledge of the women in Europe and many of them came through India having observed the women in Hindu and Islamic societies

Hence their evidence is all the more valuable. The recurring comments made by these widely traveled visitors on the women of Sri Lanka have evoked our curiosity to conduct this inquiry. The discussion that follows will deal with condition that prevailed up to the middle of the nineteenth century. Prior to this our sources are so meager that we cannot detect any major social changes. After this, due to the impact of Western imperialism, commercial enterprise and Christian missionary activity, incipient changes in the traditional structures become perceptible.

It is only in European writings that one finds lengthy accounts of the social conditions prevailing in the island. The indigenous literature, being mainly religious, lacks information regarding mundane topics like women. But from circumstantial evidence one could surmise that the liberal attitude towards women in Sri Lanka is a trend that has continued from the remote past. When one thinks of women in the traditional East, the picture that comes to our minds is that of the veiled women of Islamic societies, the zenanas where high class Indian ladies lived in seclusion, the harems of Imperial china where lived thousands of royal concubines guarded by eunuchs, the devadasis who in the name of God were forced into a life of religious prostitution; all manifesting different aspects of the exploitation of women in the East.

It is little known that there were societies in Asia where the position of women was a favorable one, judging even from modern standards. Thailand and Burma too belong to this category.

In those instances also we have based our conclusions mainly on the observations of Europeans who lived in these two countries in various capacities in the 19th and 20th centuries. R. Grant Brown, who was a revenue officer for 28 years in Burma (1889-1917) has remarked,

> *"Every writer on Burma has commented on the remarkable degree of independence attained by the women. Their position is more surprising in view of the subjection and seclusion of wives and daughters in the neighboring countries of India and China..."*

A British envoy to the Court of Ava was struck by the equal treatment accorded even to royal ladies.

"The queen sat with the king on the throne to receive the embassy. They are referred to as 'the two sovereign Lords'. It is not extraordinary to the Burmans for with them, generally speaking, woman are more nearly upon an equality with the stronger sex than among any other Eastern people of consideration."3

Lieutenant General Albert Fytche, Late Chief Commissioner of British Burma and Agent to the Viceroy and Governor General of India, wrote in 1878,

"Unlike the distrustful and suspicious Hindus and Mohammedans, woman holds among them a position of perfect freedom and independence. She is, with them, not the mere slave of passion, but has equal rights and is the recognized and duly honored helpmate of man, and in fact bears a more prominent share in the transactions of the more ordinary affairs of life than in the case perhaps with any other people, either eastern or western."

Further inquiries have revealed that in Thailand too, though not to the same extent, the women enjoyed considerable liberty. For instance, J.G.D. Campbell,5 Educational Adviser to the Government of Siam wrote in 1902,

"In Siam at any rate whatever be the causes, the position of women in on the whole a healthy one, and contrasts favorably with that among most other Oriental people. No one can have been many days in Bangkok without being struck by the robust physique and erect bearing of the ordinary woman... It can be said of Buddhism that its influence has at least been all on the right side; and when we remember the thousand arguments that have been advanced in the name of both religion and morality to degrade and debase the weaker sex, this is indeed saying much to its credit."

Sir Charles Bell, British Political Representative in Tibet, Bhutan and Sikkim, writes in 1928, "When a traveler enters

Tibet from the neighboring nations of India and China few things impress him more vigorously or more deeply than the position of the Tibetan woman. They are not kept in seclusion as are Indian women. Accustomed to mix with the other sex throughout their lives, they are at ease with men and can hold their own as well as any women in the world." Bell continues, "And the solid fact remains that in Buddhist countries women hold a remarkably good position. Burma, Ceylon and Tibet exhibit the same picture."6

These comments on the freedom and independence enjoyed by the women in certain pre-industrialized and sometimes isolated Asian societies are startling. It is not suggested that in any of these countries, Sri Lanka, Burma and Thailand, the women are on a par with the men both in theory and practice. But they have been favorably compared with the women of the neighboring countries of India and China, where Hindu, Confucian and Islamic doctrines held sway. This statement may appear contradictory for Burma and Thailand were synthesis of Indic and Sinic civilizations. In Sri Lanka too the impact of Hinduism was very strong. The question arises as to how the situation with regard to women in those three societies should be different from the major cultures of Asia. The common feature predominating in those countries is that they are intensely Buddhist. It is tempting therefore to conclude that Buddhism has helped to better the position of women in Sri Lanka, Burma and Thailand.

This conclusion would take us back to the question of the Buddhist attitude towards women and how it differs from that of other religions. Examining the position in ancient India it is clear from the evidence in the Rigveda, the earliest literature of the Indo-Aryans, that women held an honorable place in early Indian society. There were a few Rigvedic hymns composed by women. Women had access to the highest knowledge and could participate in all religious ceremonies. In domestic life too she was respected and there is no suggestion of seclusion of women and child marriage. Later when the priestly Brahmans dominated society and religion lost its spontaneity and became a mass of ritual, we see a downward trend in the position accorded to women.

The most relentless of the Brahman law givers was Manu whose Code of Laws is the most anti-feminist literature one could find. At the outset Manu deprived woman of her religious rights and spiritual life. "Sudras, slaves and women" were prohibited from reading the Vedas. A woman could not attain heaven through any merit of her own. She could not worship or perform a sacrifice by herself. She could reach heaven only through implicit obedience to her husband, be he debauched or devoid of all virtues. Having thus denied her any kind of spiritual and intellectual nourishment, Manu elaborated the myth that all women were sinful and prone to evil. "Neither shame nor decorum, nor honesty, nor timidity", says Manu, "is the cause of a woman's chastity, but the want of a suitor alone". She should therefore be kept under constant vigilance: and the best way to do it was to keep her occupied in the tasks of motherhood and domestic duties so that she has no time for mischief. Despite this denigration there was always in Indian thought an idealization of motherhood and a glorification of the feminine concept. But in actual practice, it could be said by and large, Manu's reputed Code of Laws did influence social attitudes towards women, at least in the higher rungs of society.

It is against this background that one has to view the impact of Buddhism in the 5th century B.C. It is not suggested that the Buddha inaugurated a campaign for the liberation of Indian womanhood. But he did succeed in creating a minor stir against Brahman dogma and superstition. He condemned the caste structure dominated by the Brahman, excessive ritualism and sacrifice. He denied the existence of a Godhead and emphasized emancipation by individual effort. The basic doctrine of Buddhism, salvation by one's own effort, presupposes the spiritual equality of all beings, male-and female. This should mitigate against the exclusive supremacy of the male.

It needed a man of considerable courage and a rebellious spirit to pronounce a way of life that placed woman on a level of near equality to man. The Buddha saw the spiritual potential of both men and women and founded after considerable hesitation the Order of Bhikkhunis or Nuns, one of the earliest organizations for women. The Sasana or Church consisted of the Bhikkhus (Monks), Bhikkhunis (Nuns), laymen and laywomen so that the women were not left out of any sphere of religious activity. The highest spiritual states were within the reach of both men and women and the latter needed no masculine assistance or priestly intermediary to achieve them. We could therefore agree with I.B. Horner when she says Buddhism accorded to women a position approximating to equality.

Moving from the sphere of philosophy to domestic life one notices a change of attitude when we come to Buddhist times. In all patriarchal societies the desire for male offspring is very strong for the continuance of the patrilineage and, in the case of Hindus, for the due performance of funeral rites. For only a son could carry out the funeral rites of his father and thus ensure future happiness of the deceased. This was so crucial to the Hindu that the law allowed a sonless wife to be superseded by a second or a third one or even turned out of the house. It is said "through a son he conquers the world and though a son's son he attains immortality."

As a result of this belief the birth of a daughter was the cause for lamentation. In Buddhism future happiness does not depend on funeral rites but on the actions of the deceased. The Buddhist funeral ceremony is a very simple one which could be performed by the widow, daughter or any one on the spot and the presence of a son is not compulsory. There is no ritual or ceremonial need for a son and the birth of a daughter need not be a cause for grief. It is well known that the Buddha consoled king Pasenadi who came to him grieving that his queen, Mallika, had given birth to a daughter. "A female offspring, O king, may prove even nobler than a male..." a revolutionary statement for his time. Despite the spiritual quality of the sexes and the fact that a son is not an absolute necessity in securing happiness in the after life, yet even in Buddhist societies there is a preference for male offspring even today, so potent is the ideology of male superiority.

Marriage and family are basic institutions in all societies whether primitive or modern and the position of woman in a particular society is influence by and expressed in the status she holds within these institutions. Has she got the same rights as her husband to dissolve the marriage bond? Has she the right to remarry or is this a man's privilege? The answers to these questions will undoubtedly determine the position accorded to women in any society.

Let us examine the Buddhist attitude to the question. In Buddhism, unlike Christianity and Hinduism, marriage is not a sacrament. It is purely a secular affair and the monks do not participate in it. In Sri Lanka, Thailand and Burma there is a good deal of ceremony, feasting and merry-making connected with the event but these are not of a religious nature. Sometimes monks are invited to partake of alms and they in turn bless the couple. Although there are no vows or rituals involved in the event of a marriage, the Buddha has laid down in the Sigalovada Sutta the duties of a husband and wife:

> *"In five ways should a wife as Western quarter, be ministered to by her husband: by respect, by courtesy, by faithfulness, by handing over authority to her, by*

providing her with ornaments. In these five ways does the wife minister to by her husband as the Western quarter, love him: her duties are well-performed by hospitality to kin of both, by faithfulness, by watching over the goods he brings and by skill and industry in discharging all business."

The significant point here is that the Buddha's injunctions are bilateral; the marital relationship is a reciprocal one with mutual rights and obligations. This was a momentous departure from ideas prevailing at the time. For instance Manu says, "Offspring, the due performance of happiness and heavenly bliss for one's ancestors and oneself depends on one's wife alone."

Confucius, an older contemporary of the Buddha, spoke in the same tone: "in this way when the deferential obedience of the wife was complete, the internal harmony was secured, and a long continuance of the family could be reckoned with." Confucius gives in detail the duties of the son to the father, the wife to the husband and the daughter-in-law to the mother-in-law but never vice-versa; so that the wife had only duties and obligations and the husband only rights and privileges.

According to the injunctions of the Buddha given in the Sigalovada Sutta, which deals with domestic duties, every relationship was a reciprocal one whether it be between husband and wife, parent and child, or master and servant. Ideally, therefore, among Buddhists, marriage is a contract between equals.

However it does not necessarily follow that social practice conforms to theory. The egalitarian ideals of Buddhism appear to have been impotent against the universal ideology of masculine superiority. The doctrine of Karma and Rebirth, one of the fundamental tenets of Buddhism, has been interpreted to prove the inherent superiority of the male.

According to the law of Karma, one's actions in the past will determine one's position of wealth, power, talent and even sex in future births. One is reborn a woman because of one's bad Karma. Thus the subordination of women is given a religious sanction. It is not unusual even in Sri Lanka for women, after doing a meritorious deed, to aspire to be redeemed from womanhood and be reborn as a man in future. Despite the remarkable degree of sexual equality in Burman society, all women recite as a part of their Buddhist devotions the following prayer: "I pray that I may be reborn as a male in a future existence."

In Thailand in 1399 A.D., the Queen Mother founded a monastery and commemorated the event in an inscription in which she requested, "By the power of my merit, may I be reborn as a male...". Several examples could be quoted from the popular parlance of all three societies to show that even women, whatever their station, have accepted the idea of female inferiority and this has influenced the husband-wife relationship in varying degrees in the societies concerned. In Sri Lanka where this idea is least perceptible, it is considered becoming even in modern times to maintain a facade of husband domination.

The wifely control is unobtrusive and subtle. This ambivalent attitude is more pronounced in Burma where women are a specially privileged lot. They control the family economy; socially, politically and legally they are on a par with men. But the wife makes a show of deference to the husband which in itself is no measure of male dominance but an adaptation to a cultural norm.

On the other hand, the fact that men could have multiple spouses whereas the women were restricted to one, placed the husband in a privileged position. The reverse was true in Sri Lanka where polygamy was unknown except in the royal family, polyandry was practiced (though not widespread) till recent times. In traditional Thailand the subordination of the wife in the family hierarchy was sanctioned by law. Till 1935 polygyny was legally recognized.

> *"Fundamental to the family law in the Law Code of 1805 was the conjugal power of the husband, which meant that he managed the property held jointly by the spouses, that he could sell his wife of give her away and that he could administer bodily punishment to her, provided the degree of punishment was in proportion to the misdeed."*

From the nature of the marriage contract one passes on to the question whether both parties had the same facilities for terminating the contract. It is seen that in most cultures the woman is irretrievably bound by the chains of matrimony while the man can shed his shackles with ease. The Confucian code of discipline provides the husband with several grounds for divorce. Not only leprosy and sterility, even disobedience and garrulity were valid reasons to get rid of a wife. Among the Hindus marriage was an indissoluble sacrament for the woman, while the man had the right to remarry even when the first wife was alive. Says Manu, "A barren wife may be superseded in the 8th year. She whose children all die in the 10th, she who bears only daughters in the 11th, but she who is quarrelsome without delay." In addition a man could abandon a blemished, diseased or deflowered wife. Under Islamic law the contract may be dissolved by the husband at his will without the intervention of a court and without assigning any cause. But a wife cannot divorce herself from her husband without his consent except under a contract made before or after marriage. If the conditions of the contract are not opposed to Muslim law then the divorce will take effect.

In Buddhism marriage received no religious sanction and in the absence of a Buddhist legal code comparable to the Laws of Manu or the Sharia Law of the Muslims, the dissolution the marriage contract was settled by the individuals concerned or their families. With regard to Sri Lanka, there is a document dated 1769 which gives an orthodox and official view on the subject. The Dutch who were ruling the maritime provinces of Sri Lanka wished to codify the laws and customs of the island. The Dutch Governor I.W. Falck sent a series of questions to the eminent monks of Kandy and the answers to these are given in the document known as the Lakrajalosirita. The governor raised the question whether divorce was permitted among the Sinhalese. The reply was,

> *"A man and a woman who have been united in marriage with the knowledge of their parents and relations and according to the Sinhala custom cannot become separated at their own pleasure. If a man wishes to obtain a divorce it must be by proving that his wife, failing in the reverence and respect due to a husband, has spoken to him in an unbecoming manner; or that she has lavished her affection on another and spends his earning on him, and if her improper conduct is proved before a court of justice he will be permitted to abandon her."*

The next question is for what faults on the part of the husband may the wife sue for and obtain a divorce from him. The Bhikkhus reply,

> *"If being destitute of love and affection for his wife, he withholds from her the wearing apparel and ornaments suitable to her rank; if he does not provide her with food of such a quality as she has a right to; if he neglects to acquire money by agriculture, commerce and other honorable means; if associating with other women, he squanders his property upon them; if he makes a practice of committing other improper and degrading acts such as stealing, lying or drinking intoxicating liquors, if he treats his wife as a slave and at the same times behaves*

respectfully to other women, on proof of his delinquency before the above mentioned court, the wife may obtain a divorce."

The significant point is that even in theory the Sinhala laws were equally applicable and binding to both husband and wife. One clearly sees the influence of the injunctions of the Sigalovada Sutta in the development of these institutions.

However, litigation being a tedious process then as now, it is unlikely that the average Sinhalese of the 19th century resorted to this lengthy judicial procedure. The Lakrajalosirita was written by Buddhist monks for the information of a foreigner, and judging from the rest of the document they tried to depict ideal conditions. Only the very well-to-do could afford the luxury of a court case. A more realistic account has been left by Robert Knox who spent 19 years in the company of poor peasants:

"But their marriages are but of little force and validity for if they disagree and mislike one another they part without disgrace. Yet it stands firmer for the Man than for the Woman: howbeit they do leave on the other at their pleasure."

According to Sinhala laws of the 18th century the wife was treated very liberally at the time of divorce. She got back all the wealth that her parents gave her at the time of marriage and half of all the property acquired by the couple after marriage. Also she was given a sum of money sufficient to cover her expenses for the next six months. It is worthy of note that in Sri Lanka prior to European occupation both sexes had equal facilities for divorce, both in theory and in practice. The situation changed, however, with the impact of Christianity and the introduction of Roman Dutch Law by the Hollanders in the areas under their control.

In traditional Burma too a code of divorce provided for ill assorted unions. Where there was a mutual desire for separation due to incompatibility-or other causes, parties can divorce each other by an equal division of property. If one is unwilling the other is free to go provided all property is left behind. A woman can demand a divorce if her husband ill-treats her or if he cannot maintain her; and a man in case of sterility or infidelity of the wife. Another method, not uncommon, is for the aggrieved party to seek refuge in monastic life; for this would at once dissolve the marriage bond. This easy availability of divorce in Burma has been condemned by Father Bigandet, the Roman Catholic Bishop of Rangoon as "damnable laxity". Despite this censure, it is said that this easy and equal facility for divorce has rendered the Burman spouses more forbearing and that serious connubial quarrels are rare among them.

In Thailand although women had legal disabilities, they could initiate divorce proceedings which enabled them to escape from a tyrannous husband. As far back as 1687 the French envoy to the Siamese court observed,

> *"The Husband is naturally the Master of Divorce but he never refuseth it to his wife when she absolutely desires it. He restores her portion to her and their children are divided among them in this manner..."*

Although the conjugal power of the husband was fundamental to the 1805 Code, yet the wife's right to divorce was preserved and she was treated generously when the marriage was annulled.

Moving on to the question of the remarriage of widows and divorcees, one notices that in certain societies the wives were regarded as the personal property of their husbands. As such the custom of slaying, sacrificing or burying women alive to accompany their deceased husbands along with their belongings has been found in many lands as far removed as America, Africa and India. The best known example is the soti puja or self immolation of high-caste Hindu widows. This custom which was unknown in the Rigveda, developed later: it was never very widespread but there were isolated instances continuing even up to early British times. The British had to introduce legislation to prevent it. Among the Hindus a widow was expected to lead a life of severe austerity and strict celibacy for she was bonded to her dead husband. Further she lost her social and religious status and was considered an unlucky person. The question of the remarriage of divorcees did not arise because a Hindu wife could not repudiate her husband; even if she was rejected by the latter she had to remain celibate.

In Buddhism death is considered a natural and inevitable end. As a result a woman suffers no moral degradation on account of her widowhood. Her social status is not altered in any way. In Buddhist societies she does not have to advertise her widowhood by shaving her head and relinquishing her ornaments. She is not forced to fast on specific days and sleep on hard floors for self-mortification has no place in Buddhism. Nor does she have to absent herself from ceremonies and auspicious events. Above all there is no religious barrier to her remarriage. The remarriage of rejected wives is also known in Buddhist literature.

Women whose marriages break up were free to remarry with no stigma attached,..."But if they chance to mislike one another and part asunder... then she is fit for another man, being as they account never the worse for wearing." Even the Lakrajalosirita, which gives an orthodox Buddhist view, permits the remarriage of women after separation from their spouses. It was common even in the highest rungs of society. In Burma and Thailand too women had the right to remarry after divorce. As far back as 1687 La Loubere the French envoy noticed that in Thailand, "After the Divorce both can remarry and the woman can remarry on the very day of the Divorce."

It is clear, therefore, that Buddhism has saved the daughter from indignity, elevated the wife to a position approximating to equality and retrieved the widow from abject misery.

The social freedom that women enjoyed in Buddhist societies, above everything else, has evoked from Western observers the comments that we have quoted earlier in this paper. It is not so much the equality of status but the complete desegregation of the sexes, that has distinguished the women in Buddhist societies from those of the Middle East, the Far East and the Indian subcontinent. Segregation of the sexes only leads to the seclusion and confinement of women behind veils and walls.

The Confucian code lays down detailed rules on how men and women should behave in each other's presence. Manu went to the furthest extreme of segregation by warning that one should not remain in a lonely palace even with one's own mother and sister. Sexual segregation pervades all aspects of life in Islamic society.

In early Buddhist literature one sees a free intermingling of the sexes. The celibate monks and nuns had separate quarters, yet the cloister was not cut off from the rest of the world. It is recorded that the Buddha had long conversations with his female disciples.

The devout benefactress Visakha frequented the monastery decked in all her finery, and accompanied by a maid servant she attended to the needs of the monks. Her clothes and ornaments were the talk of the town, yet neither the Buddha nor the monks dissuaded her from wearing them. It was after she developed in insight and asceticism that she voluntarily relinquished her ornaments.

This free and liberal attitude certainly had its impact on the behavior of both men and women in Buddhist societies. In Sri Lanka in the 17th century, "the Men are not Jealous of their Wives for the greatest Ladies in the land will frequently talk and discourse with any Men they please, although their Husbands be in presence."

It has been remarked that the women visited places of worship always dressed in their best attire. This is quite a contrast to the stand taken by Manu according to whom the love of ornamentation was an evil attribute of women; and the Koranic injunction that the pious woman should hide all beauty and ornamentation behind the veil. Burmese women of all ranks went unveiled and ornamented and added color to all occasions, though flanked by India and China, where customs such as purdah and foot binding prevailed. In Thailand it has been noticed that the women of the upper classes, though by no means confined to lives of strict seclusion, did not appear much in public.

In conclusion we could say that the secular nature of the marriage contract, the facility to divorce, the right to remarry, the desegregation of the sexes and above all else the right to inherit, own and dispose of property without let or hindrance from the husband, have all contributed to the alleviation of the lot of women in Buddhist societies. Conflicting with the Buddhist ethos and negating its effects in varying degrees is the universal ideology of masculine superiority. So that in all three societies - Sri Lanka, Thailand, Burma - there is an ambivalence in the attitudes towards women. Yet their position is certainly better than in any of the major cultures of Asia.

6

Female Buddhas and Bodhisattvas according to Tibetan Buddhist Tradition

The enlightened women or female figures named below all come from Vajrayana or "Tibetan" Buddhism, the school of Mahayana which originated in India and later moved to Tibet and the other Himalayan countries. Hence, most figures are identified first by their Sanskrit name, with the alternate Tibetan form appearing in parentheses. When it is the other way about, e.g. Achi Chökyi Drolma, Machig Labdrön and Palden Lhamo, it is because their practices developed or were practised principally in Tibet.

I have also indicated the type of deity each is, i.e.

- a yidam -- an enlightened meditational deity who embodies the union of wisdom and compassion, yet is not separate from the meditator
- a guru -- usually the founder or holder of a lineage; a fully realised being whom one identifies wholly with one's spiritual guide
- a Dharma protector -- usually portrayed as an enlightened being in wrathful form, a protector's primary function is to eliminate the spiritual obstacles hindering the practitioner

- a historical figure -- someone who lived as a female human being on this earth and can be placed historically according to tradition

So what's a thangka?

A thangka (pronounced tonka, as in tonka bean) is a Tibetan painting on cloth, stored scroll-fashion when travelling. For those who wish to learn more about what thangkas are and how they are created, the Dharmapala Centre in Bremen, Germany has an excellent English-language page which explains the process.

MARA

Centuries ago the coming Buddha sat under the Bodhi-tree and vowed not to move until he learned to eradicate suffering, unfolding Anuttara Samyak Sambodhi, the Consumation of Incomparable Enlightenment. But Mara, the personification of evil, tried to usurp his plans by sending his three daughters Tanha (desire), Raga (lust), and Arati (aversion), to seduce him and break his concentration. However, the coming Buddha was too strong for Mara. (source)

In Buddhism Mara is the lord of misfortune, sin, destruction and Death. Mara is the ruler of desire and death, the two evils that chain man to the wheel of ceaseless rebirth. Mara reviles man, blinds him, guides him toward sensuous desires; once man is in his bondage, Mara is free to destroy him.

Buddhist tradition holds that Buddha encountered Mara on several occasions. When he abandoned the traditional ascetic practices of Hinduism, Mara reproached him for straying from the path of purity. Mara later reappeared as a Brahmin, criticising him for neglecting the techniques of the yogins. At another time, Mara persuades householders in a village to refuse to give alms to the Buddha. Mara also accuses Buddha of sleeping too much, and not keeping busy like the villagers.

In a famous incident similar to the temptation of Jesus in the Christian religion, Mara urges Buddha to become a universal king and establish a great empire in which men can live in peace. He reminds Buddha that he can turn the Himalayas into gold if he but wishes so that all men will become rich. Buddha replies that a single man's wants are so insatiable that even two such golden mountains would fail to satisfy him."

While Mara is unable to subjugate Buddha, he is more successful with Buddha's followers, even approaching the Buddha's own brother, Ananda. As the source of evil, he causes misunderstanding between teachers and pupils, casts doubt on the value of Buddha's sayings by calling them nothing but poetry, or encourages monks to waste their time on abstruse speculations. Worse, he appears in the guise of a monk, nun, relative or prominent Brahmin, bringing false news that a disciple is destined to be a new Buddha. If the disciple succumbs to the temptation, he will be filled with sinful pride. Mara could even appear in the form of Gautama Buddha in order to confuse Buddhists or lead them astray.

Mara is lord of all men who are bound by sense desires. His origin, according to Theravada commentators, was as a rebellious prince who seized control of our world from the supreme god of the highest heaven. As prince of this world, Mara can boast of possessing great majesty and influence. Though he has only a spirit body, he is endowed with the five modes of sensual pleasure, has plenty to eat and drink, and lives to amuse himself.

Many Buddhist scholars imply that Buddha's references to Mara are mere figures of of speech (1); but the Buddhist texts do not necessarily imply anything of the sort. In

Theravada countries, veneration of good spirits, the placation of evil spirits, and Consulting Mediums are characteristic Buddhist practices. For example, the Burmese hang a coconut tied with a bit of red cloth near their home altars as an offering to the spirits. Special dances are also performed during the winter harvest season, during which a participant becomes "possessed" by spirits in order to bless the crops, while some participate in diviniation by Casting Bones Even so, the following should be remembered:

The Buddha said that neither the repetition of scriptures, nor self-torture, nor sleeping on the ground, nor the repetition of prayers, penances, hymns, charms, mantras, incantations and invocations can bring the real happiness of Nirvana. Instead the Buddha emphasized the importance of making individual effort in order to achieve spiritual goals.(source)

Buddhist texts, through inference, may suggest the possibility of a specific, living prince of evil; but Budhist writers take pains to point out it has no Adam and Eve story and no doctrine of original sin. Yet for Buddhists, the present state of human existence is "fallen" in that men are caught in a web of illusion, and long for liberation. Even though, according to Buddhist theory, men have not inherited the guilt flowing from an original sin, they are still trapped in a present state of suffering as result of evil committed in numerous past lives. Buddhism and Christianity agree that man is far from what he should be and his world is subject to the control of a malicious spirit, a powerful king of desire.

In India, prior to the advent of Buddhism, Mara was a God of Love in Vedic mythology. His name is in the language of Sanskrit and literally means death. He is a God of both Sex and Death. It is the act of love that brings a person into the world and death terminates a person. Thus, this god of death and love could be interpreted as a symbol for samsara, the cycle of birth, death and rebirth. By conquering Mara the Buddha is in effect conquering samsara. Occasionally, he is refered to as the Prince of Darkness in Buddhism. See also Kali Ma- as well as the Shaman spiritual entity and sometime foe similar to Mara to the Buddha called the Ally.

One could interpret Mara as representing an 'Anti-Buddha' --- as the opposite of everything the Buddha represents, "the enemy of the Good Law." Buddhism advocates the Middle Path in between indulgence and asceticism, while Mara is a representative of the carnal pleasures. The Buddha stands for the end of death via the Death of the Ego while Mara is death. Mara is violent. Sakyamuni Buddha is peaceful.

Early on the full moon day of Kason (April) in the year 103 of the Great Era, that is, some 2551 plus years ago, the now emaciated prince sat beneath the Bodhi Tree near the big village of Senanigãma. Around the same time, Sujãtã, the daughter of a rich man from the village, was making preparations to give an offering to the tree-spirit of the Bo tree. She had sent her maid ahead to tidy up the area around the spread of the holy tree, but at the sight of the starving man seated beneath the tree the maid thought the deity had made himself visible to receive their offering in person. She ran back in great excitement to inform her mistress. Sujãtã went to the tree and gave the prince nourishment in the form of a rice-milk gruel (Madhupayasa), inturn from which, the future Buddha regained his strength and health.

Prince Siddhartha began to eat the food beneath the shadow of the tree, sitting in a meditative mood underneath the tree from early morning to sunset, with a fiery determination and an iron resolve: "Let me die. Let my body perish. Let my flesh dry up. I will not get up from this seat till I get full illumination". He plunged himself into deep meditation. At night he entered into Deep Samadhi.

The to-be Buddha's encounter with Mara begins with that meditation. The possibility of Siddhartha becoming a Buddha and being liberated from the Earthly realm was not something that Mara desired.

Mara decided to lure Shakyamuni away from his quest for Enlightenment. He beseeched the Prince to follow his duties of father, ruler and husband and to abandon the quest for liberation from the material world. It is not proper for a king to renounce the world that he rules. The best life, Mara claimed, is to "subdue the world both with arrows and with sacrifices, and from the world obtain the world of Vsava."

Mara threatened the Prince with his bow and arrow stating that he spares those who indulge in carnal pleasures. Even when the arrow was shot, Sakyamuni stirred not. After failing to lead Gautama to the path of sensual gratification Mara utilized fear in his attempt to make Sakyamuni run away from the search for liberation. Mara gathered his fiendish minions from the deepest pits to wage war with Prince Siddhartha. The ten chief Sins, the Daughters of Mara first, then the remaining children of Mara, were sent into the fray:

- Sakkaya-ditthi is translated as "personality belief". Conceit, arrogance, pride.
- Vicikiccha means "skeptical doubt' about the Buddha, the Dhamma, the Sangha.
- Silabbataparamasa means "adherence to wrongful rites, rituals and ceremonies." The Dark Sorceress.
- Kama-raga means temptation, "sensual desire," Tanha, one of the three daughters of Mara. One of The Three Poisons.
- Patigha: ill will, including feelings of hatred, anger, resentment, revulsion, dissatisfaction, aversion,

annoyance, disappointment. Arati, one of the three daughters of Mara. As hatred, another of The Three Poisons.

- Rupa-raga is "attachment to the form realms," binding ourselves to Samsara; Raga, lust, one of the three daughters of Mara.
- Arupa-raga is "attachment to the formless realms."
- Mana "conceit, arrogance, self-assertion or pride, feeling oneself to be superior to others.
- Uddhacca, self-righteousness, "restlessness," agitation of the heart, turmoil of mind.
- Avijja is translated as ignorance and delusion, especially of the Four Noble Truths. As ignorance, the last of The Three Poisons.

After each Sin failed in subverting Shakyamuni, Mara sent forth the Lords of Hell from a thousand Limbos. The weather was turbulent, the power of Chaos, Hun-tun, mirroring the anarchic behaviour of the demons and the turmoil of the conflict. See also The Ten Fetters of Buddhism.

MAITREYA

The Coming Buddha

Until recently, almost no Buddhist scholar, Western or Eastern, would term Buddhism messianic. While all books on the religion mentioned briefly the traditional hope in a Buddha-to-come, no one felt that it deserved more than passing notice. Messianism, however, has reappeared in contemporary Theravada Buddhism, especially in Burma.

According to Buddhist scripture, Gautama predicted that at some future time another Buddha would come to help men set up an ideal kingdom of righteousness and peace. The coming Buddha is called Mettaya, (Sanskrit: Maitreya) meaning "love." In Theravada temples he is portrayed as a king rather than a monk because of his role as a ruler in the new world order. Most of the time the Maitreya hope has not been a major part of Buddhist piety. However, when Theravada monks and laymen were freed from colonial subjection after World War II, in the excitement of win- ning their independence, a new age seemed at hand. If the first 2500 years was a time of toil and trial for them, the next 2500 years would be filled with dazzling victories.

In one of his speeches Dharmapala briefly explained the Maitreya hope. The present cosmic aeon is called the great good one because four Buddhas have already come and a fifth is expected when a new race of men appears. The present human race will continue to deteriorate; righteousness will gradually disappear as injustice, cruelty and lust increase. This aeon (Kaliyuga) will last for 2,500,000 years, and then will begin the dawn of a new era. Men as we know them now will gradually die off but the remnant will provide the nucleus for a better race to come. The next Buddha, declared Dharmapala, would be born at Benares in a family of Brahmin caste. With his advent a reign of perfect righteousness will commence. There will no longer be any killing, stealing, adultery, drunkenness, filth or mud huts. The cities will all be lighted; parks and gardens will abound. Then, man will enjoy heaven on earth.

Buddhists clearly distinguish between Gautama and Maitreya. In Buddhist eschatalogy, Gautama is not expected to return; Maitreya is a different person whose mission and status are identical to that of Gautama. According to the oldest texts, Buddha does not promise to come back; what he promises is that Maitreya will become the next Buddha whose success will be far greater than his own. Also, Maitreya will bring to fulfillment the Buddhist Dhamma and inaugurate an era of cosmic bliss; he will do so as a teacher and holy man. As the Dialogues of the Buddha report, Maitreya will be "fully awakened, full of wisdom and a perfect guide, himself having trodden the path to the very end; with knowledge of the worlds, unsurpassed as an educator, teacher of gods and men, an Exalted-Buddha.... From his own understanding and penetration of it, he will proclaim (the nature of) this universe...and (the nature of) living beings. And he will proclaim the teaching that is lovely in its origin, lovely in its progress, and lovely in its consummation...the higher life will be made known in all its fullness and in all its purity.... He will be the head of an order of many thousand monks, just as in the present period I (Gautama) am the head of an order of many hundred."

Since the very beginning Buddhism offered the hope for the highest kind of individual contentment based on liberation from worldly cares. Without denying this supreme goal, Buddhists today stress the value of creating a just and prosperous social order. This is the necessary prerequisite for the pursuit of the higher joys of the spirit; only in a just environment will men have the security and leisure they need for spiritual advancement. Gautama Buddha and Maitreya Buddha actually complement each other, the first reminding us of individual self-perfection, the second challenging us to bring about the messianic age of justice and material abundance for all.

Countless eons ago, Maitreya, while making many offerings, took the Bodhisattva Vows from the Tathagata Great Power (Tub chen) in the presence of many other Buddhas. From that moment on, he has guided countless sentient beings along the path of the three higher trainings (discipline, concentration and wisdom) thereby leading them through the three vehicles (shravaka, pratyekabuddha and Bodhisattva) to Enlightenment.

While practicing as a Bodhisattva, he specialized in the meditation on great love. He not only taught this path to others, but meditated on it continuously himself. He would often station himself at the gates of a city and contemplate on loving-kindness. So powerful was his meditation that people coming and going through the gates, if they would pass close enough to touch his feet, would they receive the realization of great love. This greatly pleased all the exalted beings of the ten directions. The Tathagatas rejoiced in his actions and predicted that in his future lives, as a Bodhisattva and as a Buddha, he would be known by the name "Love" (Maitreya; Jhampa). This is how he received his name.

In one lifetime he was born as one of the thousand sons of a great king. This king wanted to know in what order his sons would become Enlightened, so he put all their names into a bowl, then drew the names out of the bowl one by one. Maitreya's name was fifth and the Buddha of that age, the Tathagata Limitless Knowledge (Yon ten pa ye) predicted that he would be the fifth Buddha of the present era, Shakyamuni being the fourth.

Eventually, Maitreya advanced through all the levels of spiritual development. He achieved the tenth and highest stage of a Bodhisattva and afterwards a fully Enlightened Buddha. Having reached this level of utmost perfection, he manifested in many different aspects in countless Buddha fields, and at present his particular abode is the Pure Land of Tushita. There he imparts mahayana teachings to many countless advanced Bodhisattva disciples, and it was in Tushita that he taught his five famous texts to the great arya being Asanga.

Maitreya also gives many other teachings in accordance with the needs of different disciples. Throughout the ten directions of space he appears as countless spiritual masters, thereby leading innumerable beings along the path to full Awakening.

Eventually the time will come for Maitreya to appear as the fifth universal Buddha of this world age and turn the Wheel of Dharma for the benefit of all. This will come about in the following manner. In the future, because of the growth of delusion, the beings living in this world will degenerate. Their lifespan will decrease and be filled with much suffering. When the human life expectancy has shortened to only ten years, Maitreya will manifest in the form of a great spiritual leader and demonstrate the path of virtue. He will particularly spread the teachings on loving-kindness and, as a result, the fortune of the beings in this world will begin to change.

As they gradually give up their deluded attitudes and harmful behavior, their lifespan will increase. After a great many ages the life expectancy of humans will grow enormously and then slowly decrease again until the human lifespan is about a hundred years. According to the prophesies of all the Buddhas and his own promise, this will be the time when Maitreya Buddha will appear in this world as a universal teacher.

His father will be called The Great Compassion Brahmin (Tramze Tsang rab) and his mother The Youthful-looking One (Tsang Denma). Maitreya will be born from her side as she stands in a forest garden, and the great celestial king Indra will receive the newborn Buddha with great devotion. Immediately the baby Maitreya will take seven steps in each of the four directions, and on each spot that he places his feet, a treasure of lotuses will bloom. Then he will declare, "I am the unsurpassed savior of the world and have come to liberate all beings from their suffering. This will be my last rebirth; there will be no further reincarnations for me." Upon hearing this, all the exalted beings and spirits of the world will rejoice, performing many acts of purification and presenting magnificent offerings to him. His proud father will then take him around the city so that the citizens can also rejoice at their new treasure. Beautiful goddesses will offer him flowers and the great sages will predict that in that very life he will become a fully Enlightened Buddha.

Thereafter he will follow the life of a royal prince. When the time comes for him to be educated, Maitreya will be the foremost of four thousand and eighty students and when it is time to marry, Maitreya will have many wives with whom he will live for many years. Then a great religious festival of Brahmins will take place in his kingdom. During this festival, Maitreya will demonstrate that he has come to realize the impermanent nature of phenomena and, seeing the examples of ascetic monks, will declare his renunciation of cyclic existence and his intention to leave his royal surroundings and follow the religious way of life. This decision will so greatly shock those around him that the whole palace and all his wives will fly up into space.

Thereafter, having made his decision to abandon the royal way of life, Maitreya will depart into the forest. All the celestial beings and saints will rejoice at his resolve and will offer prayers for his success, protecting and caring for him as he meditates. Following his example, many of his wives and one thousand and forty members of his retinue together with numerous city dwellers will follow after him in great devotion and also take ordination as religious practitioners.

For seven days, Maitreya will follow the ascetic way of life, refraining from all food and drink. Then upon arising from a state of deep meditative concentration, Maitreya will receive a bowl of milk from his wife Da way Tong chen. Refreshed by this, he will assume the diamond hard cross-legged posture and make the firm determination not to rise from meditationi until Enlightenment has been achieved. That evening he will defeat all demonic interferences and negative forces of Mara and in the middle of the night will enter a state of profound absorption. Finally, with the rising sun the following morning, Maitreya, who in fact has achieved full Enlightenment many ages before, will demonstrate for the sake of his fortunate disciples the attainment of complete and perfect Buddhahood. Then, in the same manner as all Buddhas of the past, present and future, Maitreya will lead countless beings out of their suffering and along the path to spiritual Awakening.

For seven days after his demonstration of Enlightenment, Maitraya will remain in silence, observing his future disciples. Then Indra, the king of the celestial beings, will present him with a golden wheel and the universally beautiful objects of the five senses, requesting him to turn the Wheel of Dharma for the benefit of all. In response to this request, Maitreya will teach the four truths of the noble ones and thereby lead many millions of disciples to liberation.

During his long teaching career, Maitreya will turn the wheel of great teachings three times and each time countless multitudes of disciples will come to listen.

These teachings will be enormous events attracting not merely human, earth-born disciples, but many celestial beings, dakas, dakinis and beings from other realms as well. Many of those gathered to receive these teachings will immediately become Arhats, Bodhisattvas and even fully Enlightened Buddhas. By the power of his holy body, speech and mind, Maitreya will lead and satisfy all those gathered according to their individual needs and capacities. To some he will give hinayana instructions, to others he will give mahayana. In this way, he will lead countless disciples through the three vehicles to liberation and Enlightenment.

PRAJAPATI, THE FIRST BUDDHIST NUN

If anyone wanted to present Buddhism as a viciously sexist religion, they could easily do so by quoting out of context passages from numerous sutras or from more recent texts such as Shinran's wasan (poems) or the by-laws of the Shinshu-Otani-ha (Higashi Honganji's denomination)-which denies female clergy the same status as male priests. But I believe the essential spirit of Buddhism absolutely includes all beings, male and female, in its vision of enlightenment. If I did not believe in that then I would not want to be a part of this religious tradition. In this intermittent series, I hope to make it clear that women have always been involved in Buddhist history and that their role has been very crucial even if often overlooked.

The first Buddhist nun is said to be Prajapati, Shakamuni Buddha's aunt who had raised him after the death of his mother Maya. Instead of letting his dear stepmother join his Sangha when she asked to become one of his disciples, Shakamuni's response was a declaration of the mental inferiority of women, saying they lacked the capacity to understand and practice the teachings of non-attachment to self. The BCA Dharma School textbook, Long Ago in India, glosses over this harsh refusal with the argument of "a woman's place is in the home and she can be a good Buddhist there," the typical statement heard in the Japanese cultural context.

However, in the U.S., the American followers of Tibetan Buddhism have been at the forefront of dealing with women's issues and their textbook presentation of Buddha's life for young people does not shy away from quoting Shakamuni's denunciation of women. They then go on to explain why they think Shakamuni spoke that way to his own aunt. From the time he was a boy, he was taught that women were only objects, like domesticated animals trained to breed, nurture and entertain men. From his stepmother to his wife, to all the dancing girls and servants of the palace, Shakamuni as a young prince viewed women only as creatures who lived for the rewards of pleasing men. In the

Tibetan American book on Buddha's life, Shakamuni is not blamed for his sexist attitude but is recognized as someone whose cultural conditioning allowed for no other view.

Prajapati is reluctantly allowed into the Sangha after Buddha's cousin Ananda says, "Give women a chance; we cannot say for sure that they will fail unless they have a chance to study and follow the Dharma."

Although Ananda had the same cultural conditioning as his cousin, here he speaks from his awareness of impermanence, that because of continual change, the world in each moment is new and we cannot judge the present based on the conceptions of the past. One concrete instance of impermanence which shakes up Shakamuni's view of women as pets/slaves of men is the death of his father. Prajapati now stands before him stripped of her former identity as mother and wife, no longer having a man for her life to revolve around. (As most people know, the ancient Indian custom was to throw the widow on her husband's funeral pyre since her life without a man was considered useless.)

It is my feeling that Prajapati was the person who fostered Shakamuni's interest in religion. Anyone reading the life of Buddha has to wonder why the young prince becomes so resolved to be a religious seeker when his father gave him a purely materialistic upbringing. Most ministers will say Shakamuni's spiritual sensitivity came about because of his mother's death, but Maya died when he was only a week old, too young to have much of a bond to her. Although the king surely grieved over the loss of his wife, it was not long before he had the perfect replacement for Maya - her younger sister Prajapati, called in to be his new consort and the nurturer of his son.

If anyone was greatly impacted by Maya's death, it had to be Prajapati. Because of her sister's sudden death, she had to give up whatever plans and dreams she had for herself and was expected to live up to the whole kingdom's expectation to be another Maya. The experience of impermanence- that Life does not go according to our own wishes - was clearly felt by Prajapati and to learn from it and somehow go on living, she must have had to seek spiritual guidance from the religious traditions of the time. The king probably had no use for such spiritual guidance except for gaining good luck in battle and fortune-telling, but for Prajapati, she needed to seek out something to make her disrupted life meaningful.

If this view of Prajapati is true, it could explain why she was the first to ask the Buddha to become a disciple immediately after hearing his teachings, and persisted in her request even after his brusque refusal.

As for Shakamuni, he later came to appreciate more deeply the many elements that led him to his awakening, saying there were many Buddhas before him and that their legacy made his awakening possible. This legacy could not have come to him only during his six years of ascetic practice, but there must have been some prior exposure to the religious influences of his time. In his acknowledgment of this legacy, Shakamuni must have realized that the first woman he reluctantly let into the Sangha was actually his first teacher.

Obviously, Prajapati as the first nun, and the other women of the palace who joined the Sangha along with her, succeeded in breaking down Shakamuni's cultural conditioning and enabled him to see women as equal to men in their ability to grasp and practice the teachings. Shakamuni's sexist view had to have been completely eliminated by the time of the famous sutra stories of his encounters with women such as Kisa Gotami (in the tale of the mustard seed) and Queen vaidehi (Meditation Sutra). In those stories, he would have failed to relate to them if he had held any prejudices against them as women. The historical Buddha, Shakamuni, enjoyed a life of complete freedom. He did not pursue or cling to luxuries that were unessential to his basic survival, but he also did not make a big fuss trying to avoid or refuse those things when he encountered them. However, in the earliest form of Buddhism, called Theravada (also known as Hinayana), there was a conscious effort to emulate the Buddha's sparse lifestyle as closely as possible. The ever-increasing amount of rules and regulations came to be known as the Vinaya. As all scholars of Buddhism are quick to point out, there were many more rules for women than for men; in one version, there are about 250 rules for monks and 348 rules for nuns.

NUNS AND THE VINAYA

Why were nuns more restricted than monks when, in Buddha's lifetime, the Sangha had transcended society's view of women as inferior? One reason, I think, was the way society treated nuns as opposed to monks. A monk going to meditate in the woods carrying only a begging bowl of table scraps would be an unlikely target for muggers. But nuns, wherever they went, were subjected to much harassment; the verbal taunts about their chastity, which Indian society considered unnatural, sometimes escalated into physical assault. Probably because of several violent incidents, monks were asked to chaperone nuns in their various activities in and out of the nunnery. The monks may have started out in the spirit of giving assistance to their sister disciples, but the Vinaya rules requiring a male presence at the nuns' religious ceremonies only reinforced the prejudiced view that women were unable to make any kind of spiritual progress without the guidance of men.

In an English translation of the Vinaya that I looked through at Otani University, I was surprised that many of the rules for nuns were about avoiding any behavior that could be taken as sexually suggestive. Some rules about what not to do were so graphic that it read more like someone's X-rated fantasies than guidelines to feminine modesty. This aspect of the Vinaya reflects the belief in ancient India that, because women existed mainly to please men and have babies, they were much more sex-driven than men. Due to this belief, the compilers of the Vinaya felt women needed many and more specific rules about controlling their sexuality than men did.

WOMEN AS OBJECTS OF REVULSION

I think most women would agree with me that it seemed to be the monks who had a problem with sex, rather than the nuns. This would explain why a large part of Theravada texts is devoted to the depiction of women as disgusting creatures too repulsive to touch.

A good analogy to this situation is the desperate dieter trying to imagine all food as oozing, rotting substances too nauseating to eat. Since sexual desires were considered a great hindrance in the striving for enlightenment, the monks believed the only way to eliminate their desire was to make the objects of their attachment less attractive in their minds. The historical Buddha used this approach in some instances. There was a courtesan who became a Buddhist follower and donated all her wealth to the Sangha. However, many males in the Sangha were too obsessed with her beauty and reputation to see her as a fellow disciple. When she died, the Buddha had her corpse put on display for those disciples and told them to observe the process of decay so that they would see how transient the qualities of beauty and sexuality were. Towards the woman herself, though, Buddha meant no disrespect - he knew that during her last years she had been a sincere follower of the Teachings. The problem for the Theravada monks was that in psyching themselves into seeing women's bodies as repulsive, they also came to see all other aspects of women as unworthy, making it increasingly difficult for monks to relate to nuns as human beings with the same religious aspirations as they had.

THE LOST HISTORY OF THERAVADA NUNS

According to research by female scholars of early Buddhism such as I.B. Horner, there were a large number of nuns during the first few centuries after Buddha's death. However, due to the growing hostility of secular society and of the monks, nunneries were phased out and eliminated. For almost two thousand years in India, the birthplace of Buddhism, and in Sri Lanka, where it first spread, there were no ordained women. Only in recent times has there been a reappearance of Buddhist nuns inspired by their sisters in other countries.

In the feminist view of world history, the accomplishments of women have been either ignored or appropriated by male-dominated cultures. This could very well be true for the early nuns. The only surviving text of Theravada Buddhism that is positively attributed to nuns is a compilation of songs. Who knows what other works they produced that were lost when Hinduism and Islam drove Buddhism out of favor in South Asia? It is unlikely that the monks trying to keep Buddhism alive were concerned with the works of women when so many other texts needed to be saved from destruction. Yet it is a testament to the nuns' spiritual insight and expressive power that their book of songs was respected enough to be preserved through all the upheavals in South Asia.

THE POWER AND PARTICIPATION OF WOMEN IN MAHAYANA BUDDHISM

In the last installment, I talked about the early form of Buddhism called Theravada ("the elders"). This form was later called Hinayana ("small vehicle") by the movement which developed a few hundred years after Buddha's death.

This movement, known as Mahayana ("large vehicle"), grew as more and more serious seekers realized that Theravada's insistence on following hundreds of rules and suppressing physical desires was really an attachment to fixed ideas. What was desired was a path to experiencing the ultimate truth of impermanence which the Buddha taught. In Mahayana Buddhism, since discrimination between beings was a delusion that must be transcended, lay people had as much potential to be enlightened as clergy. "Lay" and "clergy" were only artificial categories created by karmic conditions. For women this meant a new opportunity to be recognized as seekers because women were less free to leave their obligations in the secular world than men.

Northern India (Ghandara)

While Theravada Buddhism became established in southern India and neighboring countries, Mahayana flourished in northern India. This region, called Ghandara, was active in the commerce along the route between the Mediterranean and China known as the Silk Road. With the interaction between people of various cultural backgrounds along the Silk Road, the people of Central Asia in the early centuries (A.D.) were more cosmopolitan than traditional. (Ghandara Buddhist sculptures are easily recognized for their Greco-Roman characteristics.) In the rising merchant class, it was the women who were very involved in supporting Buddhist temples. It may be crass to say, but because women were in a position of economic power, Buddhist institutions had to pay attention to their spiritual needs. This explains the emphasis on sutras featuring women such as the Meditation Sutra and the Queen Srimala Sutra.

China

Mahayana Buddhism spread to China from Central Asia. In China, one of the most powerful champions of Buddhism was the Empress Wu (late 7th century). She knew that a woman seizing control of the throne went against Confucian tradition, so she used Buddhist scriptures to justify her rule. Although she was ruthlessly using Buddhism for her own political gain, the new sutras which declared the spiritual potential of women benefited the nuns in various Chinese sects. It was not uncommon for nuns to practice and work alongside monks in the monasteries, and for male and female clergy to participate together in rituals. In Chinese temples, nuns enjoyed a high degree of respect and equality, a situation that was not to be in Japan.

Japan

Ironically, when Buddhism was first established in Japan in the 6th century, the three sutras emphasized by Prince Shotoku were the Lotus Sutra, Vimalakirti Sutra and the Queen Srimala Sutra. The latter two described the acceptance in Buddha's time of female seekers as being the equal of men.

In one episode of the Vimalakirti Sutra, a woman creates the illusion of changing bodies with one of the Buddha's disciples in order to prove that the physical form of a person has nothing to do with their spiritual insight. In doing this, the woman teaches the disciple that his prejudice against women was an attachment to fixed ideas, which goes against the basic Mahayana teaching of transcending artificial categories. (I have not read the Queen Srimala Sutra, but an English translation was published a few years ago.)

Unfortunately for women in Japan, a certain episode in the Lotus Sutra was used to justify discrimination against them in Buddhist institutions. In that episode, the Princess Naga, despite her devoted practice, is told she cannot attain enlightenment because her -defiled female body is a hindrance. However, when she proves how earnestly she follows the Buddha's teachings, she is "rewarded" with the sudden transformation into a male.

During the Heian period in Japan, women produced honored literary works like The Tale of Genji. After that however, the position of women steadily declined. By the Kamakura period of Shinran's day, nuns were segregated from monks, and all women, clerical and lay, were out of consideration for enlightenment unless they could repeat the "miracle" of Princess Naga.

So profound is Amida's great compassion

That, manifesting inconceivable Buddha-wisdom,

The Buddha established the Vow of transformation into men,

Thereby vowing to enable women to attain Buddhahood

-From Jodo Wasan (p. 341, The Collected Works of Shinran, Vol. 1,

Dennis Hirota et. al., trans., Kyoto: Jodo Shinshu Hongwanji-ha, 1997)

According to the ceremonial rulebooks for priests, the above wasan (type of Japanese verse) is supposed to be chanted at the funerals for women, but there was considerable objection to the practice in Japan and most temples in America tend to chant a more standard wasan at funerals regardless of the deceased's gender. But the above wasan is important in revealing how Shinran felt about women who were very much alive.

In the Chinese version of the Immeasurable Life Sutra (also known as the Larger Sukhavativyuha Sutra), there are 48 vows made by the seeker Dharmakara to his teacher

Lokesvararaja. The most essential of these is the 18th vow, known as Hongan (main-vow), where Dharmakara proclaims that his enlightenment cannot be complete unless he can be called by the Name "Namu Amida Butsu" (meaning, the one who bows down, namu, to all beings, Amida, as enlightened, Butsu).

In the same spirit of Hongan's reverent view of all beings as existing in the state of enlightenment (Pure Land), the other vows deal with overcoming specific forms of discrimination which prevent us from seeing certain people as Pure Land residents. For example, vow #3 deals with racism ("all skin colors will be seen as glowing like precious gold") and vow #38 deals with dress codes ("all garments will be considered acceptable for Buddhas to wear no matter how torn, discolored or dirty").

Although the 35th vow represents Dharmakara's overcoming of his sexist view, in Japanese Buddhist history, the text of the vow has been interpreted as a rationale for discrimination against women. One widely accepted translation reads:

> *"If...women of the [Buddha-worlds] who, having heard my Name, rejoice in faith, awaken aspiration for Enlightenment, and wish to renounce womanhood* should be reborn again as women**, may I not attain perfect Enlightenment." (p. 37, The Three Pure Land Sutras, Hisao Inagaki, trans., Berkeley: Numata Center, 1995)*

In the above interpretation, life as a woman is a terrible state of existence that must be renounced and avoided in future rebirths in order to attain enlightenment. You can see how this became a justification for Buddhist sects to limit the role of women in the temples. Yet at the same time, the men in control assured women that their contributions of money and labor to the temples were not in vain since they still had a future chance of salvation. With this attitude directed at them, women felt unworthy of enlightenment because of their female bodies. It was sad to read in one book about Japanese Buddhism that the writer overheard one female temple member say to another while hard at work at a benefit function, "I really hate being a woman, don't you?"

During my studies in Japan, I found there is a different way of interpreting the 35th vow. One of my professors at Otani University, Akira Hataya, said the use of the word nyonin in Chinese translations of Buddhist texts, though normally read as a compound noun "female-person" (i.e., woman), could also be read as an adjective and noun memeshii hito, "effeminate (weak, wimpy) person," referring to either a man or a woman. From this, I came to feel that Buddhist texts are not trying to exclude women from the path to enlightenment, but rather the Teachings admonish both sexes not to fall into the negative traits stereotyped as "feminine" - that is, being cowardly, manipulative, or parasitic on others. There are plenty of passages in the sutras which encourage both sexes to emulate the positive aspects of femininity - to be nurturing, compassionate and sensitive towards others.

From ancient times to the present, women much more than men have been relegated to the role of "sex object," existing only to be pleasing to men's sight and other senses. The woman who seeks enlightenment, however, must break free of the mad pursuit to live up to that stereotype, and see that she is not just an object for others' pleasure. In other words, in the enlightened world, the Pure Land, women will be seen and see themselves as human beings equal to men, not as inferior objects. See how different the 35th vow sounds when we put in an objectifying term such as "bimbo."

"May I attain the highest enlightenment only when women who hear my Name realize how demeaning it

is to be seen as a bimbo and in their new life of seeking the Dharma, their joy and faith will keep them from ever wanting to be seen as a bimbo again."

Shinran in his day did not have the benefit of such a progressive interpretation, but he came to a similar conclusion through his own experience of the Nembutsu. Shinran did not question the prevailing belief that women were too defiled to be enlightened. However, to think that a woman's body would be more corrupt than a man's did not matter much when Shinran already felt that the human body itself was irredeemably corrupt - full of desires and angers which cannot be quieted for more than a few moments at a time. He questioned the claims that there were actual people who totally conquered their bodily functions and manifested the so-called "marks of the Buddha" (such as special swirls on the feet and the retraction of private parts).

According to Shinran, complete enlightenment cannot be attained as long as we exist as biological creatures, yet once we awaken to the truth that our individual lives are embraced by Infinite Life (Amida), it means complete enlightenment will definitely occur. Shinran often uses the phrase, "equal to Maitreya," meaning that despite our defiled bodies, we are on the brink of enlightenment like the prototype Maitreya, the "Buddha-to-be." To Shinran, since each "Buddha-to-be" will inevitably arrive at the Pure Land like Maitreya, they can start enjoying the benefits of enlightenment here and now, rather than waiting for the distant future.

This absorption of a future inevitability into the present moment also characterizes Shinran's attitude towards women. In the above wasan, Shinran praises Amida's power to change a being in a separate category labeled "women" to a someone in the same "Buddha-to-be" category of all men. Since Shinran believes this will definitely occur, he can consider all women as "Buddhas-to-be" equal to any man. The power of the all-encompassing Infinite Life breaks down what the people of Shinran's time saw as women's biological obstacle on the spiritual path.

I believe that due to cultural conditioning, some women may require different approaches to religion than most men, just like some Americans need to approach Buddhism differently than most Japanese. But whatever your gender, race, economic status, etc., the 48 vows in the Immeasurable Life Sutra point out that there is no discrimination against anyone on the path to spiritual truth. If anyone tries to tell you otherwise, be assured that the Buddha's words won't support them.

The role of women in religion, especially Eastern religions, is a strange one. Western religions are fairly straightforward about a women's place. For example, most Western religions (excluding the Roman Catholic Church) allow women in leadership roles within the religious community. Judaism allows women rabbis, most Christian religions allow women ministers, and even Islam, which does not allow women mullah, have had many influential female sufi's throughout Islamic history.

Women have had similar roles in Eastern religion. However, the big difference in Eastern religion is in the philosophical or scriptural attitude towards women versus the actual, "everyday role" of women.

According to the Bhagavad Gita, "...those who take shelter in Me, though they be of lower birth -- women, vaisyas (merchants), as well as sudras (workers) -- can approach the supreme destination." (Bhagavad Gita, 9:32) This places women in a spiritual role similar to that of men. However, because of the place of women in traditional Indian society, women are thought to be inferior. This is clearly expressed in the Gita in a number of chapters. Women are thought to be untrustworthy and stupid, easily corrupted (1:40), and a hindrance to men on the path to liberation (16:11- 12).

The Manu-samhita, a Hindu book that lays down "the law of the human race," explains that women should not be given freedom and should be protected at all times. According to Swami Prabhupada, the leader of the Krishna Consciousness movement, "That does not mean that women are to be kept as slaves, but they are like children. Children are not given freedom, but that does not mean they are kept as slaves." (Commentary on 16:7, Bhagavad Gita, Prabhupada translation).

This dual nature of women in Hinduism has had a major effect on Hinduism's spread. Hinduism is so entwined in Indian culture, as I have shown, that most other cultures have a difficult time assimilating Hinduism into their own society. Even when Hinduism is assimilated into a culture, such as Hindu movements in the United States, women are sure to find discrimination in not only the traditional gurus and swamis who are teaching them, but sexist commentaries deeply ingrained in religious texts.

Buddhism suffers from the opposite extreme. The Buddha originally banned women from monastic practice but later reversed his decision, allowing them to practice in separate quarters. Buddhist scriptures say very little about women, treating them as equals. In one scripture, the Visuddhi Magga, a monk asked: "Reverend Sir, have you seen a woman pass this way?" And the elder said:

> *Was it a woman, or a man That passed this way? I cannot tell. But this I know, a set of bones Is travelling upon this road. (Visuddhi Magga, Ch1. FROM: Coomaraswamy.)*

Although this verse attempts to show the equality of women on the spiritual path, there was, and is, still sexual stereotypes similar to that found in the Bhagavad Gita. Once Gautama responded to one of his disciples questions about women by saying: "Women are soon to be angered, Ananda; women are full of passion, Ananda; women are envious, Ananda; women are stupid, Ananda." (Lalitavistara Sutra, 309) Again, the problem of cultural stereotypes enters the picture. Fortunately for Buddhism, the opinions of its founder(s) were not strongly embedded in the teachings. Women, in most cases, were considered equal within the law of the Dharma. The universe treated them equally, with equal attributes and abilities, even if the male teachers occasionally mumbled their disapproval when no one was watching. (Personal Experience)

The role of women in Hindu movements in the United States has not advanced very far. Although women hold many teaching and management roles in Hindu movements, the highest role, that of spiritual master, is still held only by men. The reason for this is the same as the one used by the Gita. According to Kelly Beek, an active member in the Krisna Consciousness movement and manager of Govinda's Restaurant in San Diego, women are not well suited to be spiritual masters. Although there have been women masters in Hindu history, women tend to be emotional, and not well prepared and able to handle the stress of such a position. She knew of no female spiritual masters teaching today. (Phone Conversation, 5/9/91, 12:30 p.m.)

Buddhism is known to be less of a culturally based religion, which has helped immensely in its spread throughout the world. In more recent times women have enjoyed much freedom within Buddhism. Although Asian cultures still frown on women masters, such as in Japan and Korea, other cultures put women on a more equal basis. Buddhism in America, has greatly expanded women's role in Buddhism.

Reverend (Roshi) Jiyu-Kennet, the Abbess of Shasta Abbey, on Mount Shasta, has created a large Buddhist order throughout the Western United States and parts of Europe. Men and women monastics practice Buddhism together in an environment of equal respect and equality. Other famous female Buddhist teachers in the United States include the late Roshi Myoon Maurine Stuart who taught at the Zen Center of Syracuse. She not only taught the equality of women in Buddhism, she even demonstrated it was possible to have a "normal" life with a husband and children, and still be an effective spiritual master. (Helen Tworkow, Butsumon, Spring 1990, 15) Even San Diego has its own woman Roshi, Roshi Charlotte "Joko" Beck of the Zen Center of San Diego.

All of these female teachers received ordination and spiritual transmission from traditional Japanese male teachers. This demonstrates that Japanese Zen Masters feel that women are equal to men, even if they cannot express it in their own, male-dominated society. What this says is that the role of women in Eastern religion is based entirely on culture perspectives. Both Buddhism and Hinduism affirm the equality of women in relation with the divine, be it Buddha nature or relationship with God (Brahman). As traditional Asian Buddhist countries, such as Japan, Korea and India, develop more equality towards women, female religious teachers should become much more common. This may be just what Buddhism needs to shake it from its lethargy, and give it a boost of much needed energy. As it stands now, the United States has become the spiritual center for Buddhism, a fact that has a lot to do with the role of women in these traditions.

BUDDHISM

The ordination of women is currently and historically practiced in some Buddhist regions, such East Asia and

Taiwan, and not in others, such as India and Sri Lanka. The tradition of the ordained monastic community (sangha) began with Buddha, who established orders of Bhikkhu (monks) and later, after an initial reluctance, of Bhikkuni (nuns). The stories, sayings and deeds of some of the distinguished Bhikkhuni of early Buddhism are recorded in many places in the Pali Canon, most notably in the Therigatha. However, not only did the Buddha lay down more rules of discipline for the bhikkhuni (311 compared to the bhikkhu's 227), he also made it more difficult for them to be ordained.

The tradition flourished for centuries throughout South and East Asia, but appears to have died out in the Theravada traditions of India and Sri Lanka in the 11th century C.E. However, the Mahayana tradition, particularly in Taiwan and Hong Kong, has retained the practice, where nuns are called 'Bhik?u??' (the Sanskrit equivalent of the Pali 'Bhikkhuni'). Nuns are also found in Korea and Vietnam.

There have been some attempts in recent years to revive the tradition of women in the sangha within Theravada Buddhism in Thailand, India and Sri Lanka, with many women ordained in Sri Lanka since the late 1990s. The International Congress on Buddhist Women's Role in the Sangha: Bhikshuni Vinaya and Ordination Lineages, taking place in Germany, on July 18-20, 2007, is a turning point in reviving the Bhikkhuni lineage.

Thailand

In 1928, the Supreme Patriarch of Thailand, responding to the attempted ordination of two women, issued an edict that monks must not ordain women. The two women were reportedly arrested and jailed briefly. In a more recent challenge to the Thai sangha's ban on women, Dhammananda Bhikkhuni, previously a professor of Buddhist philosophy known as Dr Chatsumarn Kabilsingh, was controversially ordained as a nun in Sri Lanka in 2003. Despite some support inside the religious hierarchy, the sangha remains fiercely opposed to the ordination of women.

Tibetan Tradition

The 2007 International Congress on Buddhist Women's Role in the Sangha, with the support of H. H. XIVth Dalai Lama, is expected to reinstate the Gelongma (skt. Bikshuni, tib. Gelongma) lineage, having been lost, in India and Tibet, for centuries[citation needed]. It is currently only possible for women to take Rabjungma ('entering') and Getshülma ('novice') ordinations in Tibetan tradition. Gelongma ordination requires the presence of ten fully ordained people keeping the exact same vows (men's and women's vows differ slightly). Because 10 Gelongmas are required in order to ordain a new Gelongma[citation needed], the effort to reinstate the Gelongma tradition has taken a long time.

It is permissible for a Tibetan nun to receive Bikshuni ordination from another living tradition, e.g., in Vietnam. Based on this, Western nuns ordained in Tibetan tradition, like Venerable Thubten Chodron, took full ordination in another tradition, in order to revive 'Gelongma' ordination[citation needed]. The same socio-cultural reasons that make it difficult for women to be nuns will still present challenges to the first Tibetan Gelongmas.

Do Women do it Differently?

Do women take a distinctive approach to the elements of the Buddhist path? I believe they do, because our life experience differs in many respects from men's.

Girls receive early social conditioning that is, in most cases, different from the training of little boys; women encounter particular expectations, dangers, and obstacles as well as encouragement to develop specific qualities in themselves, perform certain roles, follow particular paths. Because of this conditioning, the inner life of women is bound to be different from the subjective universe of most men. Certainly women are capable of doing any work that men do, and we have the examples of female doctors, lawyers, electricians, athletes, carpenters, CEOs, spiritual teachers, ministers, scholars, and scientists too convince us that no intellectual, spiritual, or physical achievement lies outside the realm of women's abilities. But we can surmise that women in these professions may approach their work in a distinctive manner or may view its practice and significance differently from their male colleagues. In some cases women's participation may change the nature of the profession itself.

Female spiritual teachers in the Buddhist tradition have and continue to offer the teaching in innovative and often recognizably female-oriented ways.

Women may take a more psychological approach to teaching, adapting their message to the twentieth-century, psychologically-oriented conciousnesses of their students.

Women teachers may be more accepting of the expression of emotion by their students. Some women practitioners tell of spending time in male-run environments where emotions were suppressed, and then going to a female teacher who encouraged them to acknowledge and fully experience whatever strong feelings might be coming up in them.

Other women teachers do not limit themselves to the traditional forms of practice but strike out to devise new methods or incorporate elements of other traditions. At a woman-led retreat you may find yourself dancing in a circle, reaching to the sky, touching the ground. You may be led on journeys of guided imagery. You may be invited to pay particular attention to the natural environment in which you practice, noting the life of trees, animals, rocks and streams and how this is interrelated with your own life.

How have Feminists Affected American Buddhism?

Those of you who are interested in the issues raised by the most recent women's movement may wonder whether it has made a mark on the institutions and practices of American Buddhism. The answer is a definite yes.

Since the early 1980's, two groups of women have come together in Buddhist practice situations, though sometimes with difficulty: the women who had dedicated themselves early on to Buddhist practice and institutions, and the women new to Buddhism who had engaged in feminist political activism. Each group brought something crucial to the mix. Feminist women new to Buddhism insisted on equality, critique of hierarchy, identification of misogynist texts and practices, and altering of sexist language. Women with years of Buddhist practice brought patience, seasoned spiritual perspective, and a spacious view to the dialogue.

A series of conferences on Women and Buddhism, held across the country, allowed women to break out of their isolation and talk with other women and a few supportive men about the issues that concerned them. They allowed us to experience the teachings of some female Buddhist "masters" who came to give talks, and we were able to discuss volatile subjects like sexual abuse by male teachers. Women expressed their differences in perspective: creative, innovative practice versus more traditional forms; insistence on equality and nonhierarchical relationships in Buddhist centers versus a trust in the usefulness of traditional hierarchical structures; incorporation of goddess worship, shamanic and Native American elements into the practice versus a holding to the pure Buddhist forms. The conferences built understanding and trust among women Buddhist practitioners of all persuasions and gave many women the sense that they were not alone but had become part of a collective questioning of the forms within American

Buddhism. They drew strength to challenge oppressive or abusive situations when they identified them within their own Buddhist environments.

As a result of the persistent, courageous efforts of these women and others, many Buddhist institutions have become more sensitive to women's particular needs, more open to women's spiritual leadership, and less hierarchical in their structures.

One particularly dramatic contribution of feminism to Buddhism has been the shift in perspective on sexual power abuse by teachers. Through the efforts of determined women and a few men, the veil of secrecy previously obscuring the issues of sexual abuse has been drawn aside, and a lively public debate has ensued about how to approach such incidents.

While abuses still occur, there is much more openness in confronting and dealing with them. Some Buddhist teachers are making efforts to establish a code of conduct to which all Buddhist centers would agree to subscribe.

Can Women be Buddhist Leaders?

If you grew up in a Catholic household, you know well that women's participation in the hierarchy of the Catholic Church is strictly circumscribed. Again and again I have heard the discouraging story of the little girl, fired by religious zeal, who asks to be the child who assists the priest at the altar. She is told that only boys can help to celebrate the mass. When those little girls grow up, they are acutely aware that only men can be priests who give the gift of God to the community.

In many Protestant denominations, through the efforts of dedicated women activists, women ministers are ordained and routinely officiate and preach in churches. In others, the doors are still closed to full participation. In some churches women are ordained but not given the full responsibilities of ministers. Lesbian women in particular find it difficult to be accepted and empowered by Protestant denominations.

Since the late 1970's, a number of women have become rabbis in the Jewish faith, generally in the more liberal synagogues and seminaries. In Orthodox settings no women are allowed to officiate. The Conservative, Reformed, and particularly the Reconstructionist or Jewish Renewal movements do allow women to become rabbis. While female rabbis still face prejudice, more and more of them are becoming the leaders of congregations. And some Lesbian rabbis also perform rabbinical duties in synagogues.

Can Buddhist women wear the robes and carry out the duties of religious celebrants? The answer is as varied as Buddhism itself.

In most Western Buddhist settings, women perform the same religious offices as men. At a Zen monastery you will see probably an equal number of women and men wearing black robes, ringing the bells, beating the drums, and giving the dharma talks.

In Vipassana settings, there is little official hierarchy; no one even wears robes (except an occasional visiting Theravada monk or nun). Women are very visible and influential in the Vipassana establishment.

Tibetan Buddhism's attitude toward women leaders is more complex. The tradition was brought to this country by maroon-robed monks in exile from their native Tibet, and in their Western sanghas, these foreign monks remain at the top of the hierarchy. But these monks have ordained Westerners, including a very few female lamas. Each of the four separate traditions or "schools" within Tibetan Buddhism takes a somewhat different approach to hierarchy and practice. Notable Tibetan Buddhist women leaders include Pema Chodron, an American woman who heads a Tibetan Buddhist monastery in Nova Scotia, and Tsultrim Allione, who has broken away-from male-led groups to establish her own center and teaching schedule. Many other Tibetan Buddhist women hold positions of authority in the male-run centers, but always subordinate to male leaders.

Soka Gakkai is as open to women's leadership as men's. They operate from a Japanese model, in which women's and men's activities are often pursued separately.

The immigrant sanghas generally reflect the traditional gender hierarchy maintained in Asian cultures. Men are usually at the top, and women support their work. There are, or course, exceptions, as the sanghas become more Americanized. For example, a Japanese-American woman serves as a fully ordained priest in Shin Buddhism, a largely Japanese denomination.

Are there Goddesses in Buddhism?

Many contemporary women are intrigued by the idea of an ancient goddess culture, a time in prehistory in which women shared equally with men in all dimensions of public and private life. Archeological research in the Middle East has unearthed evidence of a peaceful agricultural society in which female divinities or perhaps one divinity, the Great Goddess associated with earth and the cyclical creation of all life, were venerated. According to this theory, this egalitarian, nurturing society was conquered and taken over about five thousand years ago by peoples from a more Northern, warlike society, and the centuries of patriarchal aggression and hierarchy began. The conquerors overthrew the goddesses and enthroned a single creator-god.

However, in some religions, vestiges of the early goddess figures have survived. In Christianity, the Virgin Mary can be seen as a goddess. The Virgin of Guadeloupe in Mexico

City and other great virgins hold tremendous power in their particular cultures. Female saints like Joan of Arc and Teresa of Avila, while they were actual historical figures, have accumulated almost the glamour and influence of goddesses.

In Judaism the deity is sometimes called Shekinah, a feminine name. This word is used for the comforting, more personal aspect of God. The Hebrew goddess Asherah and the Canaanite goddess Astarte were worshipped in Hebrew temples before the masculine god took over. Perhaps the Shekinah is their legacy, a concession to the need to connect with and venerate female essence.

In Buddhism a number of powerful female emanations hold sway. The two best known of these, whose images you may come across, are Kwan Yin and Tara.

If you have looked at Buddhist art, you've noticed that many representations of the Buddha or other embodiments have decidedly feminine characteristics: breasts, delicate facial features, softly draped clothing. Buddhists believe that as beings achieve more refined levels of enlightenment, the distinctions of sex and gender fall away, leaving a transgendered or genderless figure. Nevertheless, the Buddhas or other figures with breasts and sweet girlish smiles are always referred to as "he." Similarly, male Buddhist teachers who have studied with or venerated female teachers or forbears may express feminine qualities in their teachings, but they retain their conventionally masculine assumptions and sense of entitlement.

Kwan Yin

Kwan Yin (also spelled Quan Yin, Guan shih yin, Kannon, and Kwannon-sama), the Buddhist female embodiment of compassion, is the most revered goddess in Asia. She originated in China and is venerated in Japan,

Korea, and throughout Southeast Asia. In Burma, for instance, statues of the goddess of compassion can be found in almost every home. While she is a Buddhist embodiment of the highest spiritual attainment, Kwan Yin also has the wide popularity of a folk goddess.

A lovely, playful goddess, Kwan Yin grants the wishes of those who call upon her, especially women, and exerts particular power over childbirth. Her name means "She Who Harkens to the Cries of the World," for she is the one who arrives to save people from burning buildings, pluck them from train wrecks, and to offer general relief from suffering. It is Kwan Tin who listens to the voices of the poor and oppressed.

Kwan Yin came to China from India in the form of the Buddhists Avalokitesvara, the embodiment of compassion in a male form. But as she became more Chinese, she also became more womanly, until finally she took on a completely female character and appearance. Soon she was identified with various real life women who were discovered to be deities after their deaths. When Kwan Yin assumed human and Chinese identities, she achieved a widespread national following. Some scholars believe that Kwan Yin's female nature resulted from the fusion of the qualities of Avalokitesvara with the Taoist Queen Mother of the West. Others see her origin in the early Indian, later Tibetan, goddess Tara.

If you come upon statues or paintings of Kwan Yin, you will see her in one of several forms. these different embodiments of Kwan Yin derive from the Chinese appearances. the development of Kwan Yin began with Ta pei Kuan Yin (who started out in life as the Princess Miao-shan), the thousand-armed, thousand-eyed goddess of compassion (a counterpart to Avalokitesvara, who also has a thousand arms and eyes). Ta pei is later depicted with just two arms and two eyes, holding a green willow branch and a bottle of pure water or life-giving nectar, symbols of healing.

Next came Nan hai Kuan Yin, the "Kwan Yin of the South Sea," who is shown with a male and female companion and a white parrot. Sailors from the Southern port cities of China venerate her and call upon her to save them from stormy seas.

Accounts from the twelfth to the fourteenth centuries describe another manifestation, Yu-la Kuan-yin, otherwise known as "Kwan Yin with the Fish Basket," "Mr. Ma's wife," and "Kwan-Yin with Chained Bones," names deriving from the vivd stories of her arrival in people's lives. When her human embodiment died, her bones were found to be attached to each other by golden chains, a sure sign of divinity.

A surprising and provocative form of Kwan Yin was known as the "Woman of Yen-chu," a woman who gave away sex to any man who asked her, in order to free him of his unhealthy desire. She was the sensual Bodhisattva who used bodily desire to achieve enlightenment. (Learning about her, I pondered a possible connection between the Woman of Yen-chu and the temple priestesses of antiquity, whose religious duties included sexual intercourse.) Later, when the rather puritanical Confucianism became popular in China, this Kwan Yin fell into disrepute and was no longer worshipped.

Finally, there is the "White-robed Kwan Yin" (Pai-i Kuan-yin), a goddess capable of granting children. Often depicted holding a baby, she was not a mother herself but represented universal motherliness. The veneration of Kwan Yin grew to include the chanting of mantras to petition White-robed Kwan Yin to grant the male children necessary for ancestor worship and funeral rites.

For several years now, it has been my joy and privilege to lead groups of women on pilgrimages to ancient places in the world. When I travel, I take my connection to the land with me.

Growing up in a redwood forest on the Mendocino coast profoundly influenced my development. I was raised at the very end of Simpson Lane, between Caspar and Fort Bragg. The last mile of road was unpaved, and we often had to park at the bottom of the hill during the winter months and walk up to our house. I was isolated there as a child, and desperately lonely, but all around was a living cathedral of redwoods. I spent most of my childhood in that forest. I'd lie down in a circle of trees and feel something come up through me, as though the forest were embracing and nourishing me. I loved to look up at the swaying bodies and the whispering leaves, to smell the earth mold and take in the whole life of the forest. It seemed to speak a language that only I could understand. I was devastated when I discovered that the redwoods were actually finite and that people were cutting them down.

In the early sixties, with the influx of artists to Mendocino County, people came into my life who perceived the world as I did. For the first time, I realized that the language of the trees and the ocean was similar to the language of art, music and dance. This saved my life by teaching me to trust what is deep inside me.

Sacred Journeys

To live a spiritual life is to attend to the wisdom and essence that is within us. The pilgrim's journey is an inner and outer expression of the necessity to find that sacred center. The journey necessitates leaving behind our everyday life. To experience the transformation we seek we must prepare ourselves and open to the unexpected.

Crossing the Threshold between Two Worlds

The experience of journeying with a group is largely determined by how well the trip is organized. If you move around every day in order to see as much as possible, it becomes very hard to focus on the spiritual nature of a place. I have the pleasure of working with singer/songwriter Jennifer Berezan (Edge of Wonder Tours) and performance artist Alaura O'Dell (Sacred Journeys for Women) who carefully plan group journeys so that women can have the most meaningful experiences.

The pilgrimage begins the moment one decides to go on a sacred journey and continues with inner and outer preparation. Everything that arises -- every discovery, every irritation, every disappointment, every exultation -- is the journey. Each woman comes to it with her own background, and although to some degree she will encounter an ordeal, the disruption of normal routine awakens our ability to see the world in new ways.

When we fly a great distance through the air in a great metal bird, and land hours later in a far away place, we are already in a liminal or dreamlike state (some call it jet lag). the act of crossing the threshold from the known to the unknown stimulates new perceptions and awakenings that have both individual and collective dimensions. No individual viewpoint is universal; each person's perception is specific to where she's standing, but at a certain point in each trip the entire group begins to resonate together and a spirited dynamic is cultivated between the individual and the collective.

We prepare ourselves intellectually and spiritually to visit sacred sites and allow time to be there, in a meditative way. Our groups include lectures by various scholars. We take the time to meet in circles, check in, sing, meditate, dance, process our experiences with each other and develop a group intimacy. We encourage women to open their minds, hearts, and spirits to the ineffable and unpredictable. Many who travel know that amazing coincidences or serendipitous moments occur when we give up expectations and allow ourselves to enter into the mystery.The concentrated energy awakens the deep resonance of ancient memory. Although the Neolithic people who created these temples are gone, the stones still transmit their relationship to the sacred.

The Hypogeum

The Hypogeum on Malta is an extraordinary subterranean temple/tomb that was utilized for ritual and collective burial between 4000-2500 BC. It consists of thirty-three egg shaped chambers on three different levels. They were carved out of the living limestone with antler and flint tools, before the use of metals. Several central rooms are elegantly shaped to resemble the above ground temples where ceremonies related to death and regeneration probably took place. The dead were buried in chambers filled with red field soil. Later the bones were gathered and placed with thousands of other bones in special niches smeared with red ochre. In this way, the living community maintained a sacred communion with its ancestors.

The Hypogeum has phenomenal acoustics. There is a myth that only a male voice can resonate throughout the chambers. But Jennifer recorded a beautiful album there called "Returning to the Mother of Us All." (A special multicultural event will celebrate this new CD on February 6, 2000 at the Scottish Rite Temple in Oakland, California. It will also be a fundraiser for the biography I wrote of Marija Gimbutas, and for the film "Marija" being created by Donna Read and Starhawk.)

Our journeys to Malta always take place during the summer solstice or the equinoxes so we can experience the solar alignments at Mnajdra Temple. We arrive at the temple before dawn to to watch the sunrise. At the spring and fall equinox, the light of the sunrise streams through the perfect center of the entrance illuminating the head altar. At the summer solstice, the sun's rays enter at an angle and strike a specific interior stone. On several occasions we have been the only people present to experience these sacred events.

We also make special arrangements each year with the archaeological museum to do ceremonies by ourselves for an entire evening in Hagar Qim temple. This extraordinary highlight of our yearly pilgrimage is worth the entire journey. Being there, near the Mediterranean, among the ancient stones, with time to meditate, sing and enact whatever ceremony we create together -- is indescribable.

Keeping in Touch

Our entire life is a pilgrim's journey. It seems to me that one of the most important realizations is to become reconciled with the fact that we are going to die. Then, we have the possibility to wake up, to become more fully alive and to remember those things that are most important -- compassion and forgiveness.

Due to deeply shared experiences on these journeys, friendships are formed that last for years. Our intimate community is expanding. Once our inner lives have been activated, our journeys continue to unfold.

A female child may prove even to be a better offspring than a male.

Women's position in Buddhism is unique. The Buddha gave women full freedom to participate in a religious life. The Buddha was the first religious Teacher who gave this religious freedom to women. Before the Buddha, women's duties had been restricted to the kitchen; women were not even allowed to enter any temple or to recite any religious scripture. During the Buddha's time, women's position in society was very low. The Buddha was criticized by the prevailing establishment when He gave this freedom to women. His move to allow women to enter the Holy Order was extremely radical for the times. Yet the Buddha allowed women to prove themselves and to show that they too had the capacity like men to attain the highest position in the religious way of life by attaining Arahantahood. Every woman in the world must be grateful to the Buddha for showing them the real religious way of living and for giving such freedom to them for the first time in world history.

A good illustration of the prevailing attitude towards women during the Buddha's time is found in these words of Mara: 'No woman, with the two-finger wisdom (narrow)which is hers, could ever hope to reach those heights which are attained only by the sages.'

Undoubtedly, the Buddha was vehement in contradicting such attitude. The nun (bhikkhuni) to whom Mara addressed these words, gave the following reply:

'When one's mind is well concentrated and wisdom never fails, does the fact of being a woman make any difference?'

King Kosala was very disappointed when he heard that his Queen had given birth to a baby girl. He had expected a boy. To console the sad King, the Buddha said:

'A female child, O Lord of men, may prove

Even a better offspring than a male.

For she may grow up wise and virtuous,

Her husband's mother reverencing, true wife,

The boy that she may bear may do great deeds,

And rule great realms, yes, such a son

Of noble wife becomes his country's guide,'

(Samyutta Nikaya)

The Buddha has confirmed that man is not always the only wise one; woman is also wise.

Nowadays many religionists like to claim that their religions give women equal rights. We only have to look at the world around us today to see the position of women in many societies. It seems that they have no property rights, are discriminated in various fields and generally suffer abuse in many subtle forms. Even in western countries, women like the Suffragettes had to fight very hard for their rights. According to Buddhism, it is not justifiable to regard women as inferior. The Buddha Himself was born as a woman on several occasions during His previous births in Samsara and even as a women He developed the noble qualities and wisdom until He gained Enlightenment or Buddhahood.

The Buddha had gone beyond all worldly affairs, but still gave advice on good government.

The Buddha came from a warrior caste and was naturally brought into association with kings, princes and ministers. Despite His origin and association, He never resorted to the influence of political power to introduce His teaching, nor allowed His Teaching to be misused for gaining political power. But today, many politicians try to drag the Buddha's name into politics by introducing Him as a communist, capitalist, or even an imperialist. They have forgotten that the new political philosophy as we know it really developed in the West long after the Buddha's time. Those who try to make use of the good name of the Buddha for their own personal advantage must remember that the Buddha was the Supremely Enlightened One who had gone beyond all worldly concerns.

There is an inherent problem of trying to intermingle religion with politics. The basis of religion is morality, purity and faith, while that for politics is power. In the course of history, religion has often been used to give legitimacy to those in power and their exercise of that power. Religion was used to justify wars and conquests, persecutions, atrocities, rebellions, destruction of works of art and culture.

When religion is used to pander to political whims, it has to forego its high moral ideals and become debased by worldly political demands.

The thrust of the Buddha Dhamma is not directed to the creation of new political institutions and establishing political arrangements. Basically, it seeks to approach the problems of society by reforming the individuals constituting that society and by suggesting some general principles through which the society can be guided towards greater humanism, improved welfare of its members, and more equitable sharing of resources.

There is a limit to the extent to which a political system can safeguard the happiness and prosperity of its people. No political system, no matter how ideal it may appear to be, can bring about peace and happiness as long as the people in the system are dominated by greed, hatred and delusion. In addition, no matter what political system is adopted, there are certain universal factors which the members of that society will have to experience: the effects of good and bad kamma, the lack of real satisfaction or everlasting happiness in the world characterized by dukkha(unsatisfactoriness), anicca(impermanence), and anatta(egolessness). To the Buddhist, nowhere in Samsara is there real freedom, not even in the heavens or the world of Brahama.

Although a good and just political system which guarantees basic human rights and contains checks and balances to the use of power is an important condition for a happy in society, people should not fritter away their time by endlessly searching for the ultimate political system where men can be completely free, because complete freedom cannot be found in any system but only in minds which are free. To be free, people will have to look within their own minds and work towards freeing themselves from the chains of ignorance and craving. Freedom in the truest sense is only possible when a person uses Dhamma to develop his character through good speech and action and to train his mind so as to expand his mental potential and achieve his ultimate aim of enlightenment.

While recognizing the usefulness of separating religion from politics and the limitations of political systems in bringing about peace and happiness, there are several aspects of the Buddha's teaching which have close correspondence to the political arrangements of the present day. Firstly, the Buddha spoke about the equality of all human beings long before Abraham Lincoln, and that classes and castes are artificial barriers erected by society. The only classification of human beings, according to the Buddha, is based on the quality of their moral conduct. Secondly, the Buddha encouraged the spirit of social -co-operation and active participation in society. This spirit is actively promoted in the political process of modern societies. Thirdly, since no one was appointed as the Buddha's successor, the members of the Order were to be guided by the Dhamma and Vinaya, or in short, the Rule of Law. Until today very member of the Sangha is to abide by the Rule of Law which governs and guides their conduct.

Fourthly, the Buddha encouraged the spirit of consultation and the democratic process. This is shown within the community of the Order in which all members have the right to decide on matters of general concern. When a serious question arose demanding attention, the issues were put before the monks and discussed in a manner similar to the democratic parliamentary system used today. This self-governing procedure may come as a surprise to many to learn that in the assemblies of Buddhists in India 2,500 years and more ago are to be found the rudiments of the parliamentary practice of the present day.

A special officer similar to 'Mr. Speaker' was appointed to preserve the dignity of the Parliamentary Chief Whip, was also appointed to see if the quorum was secured. Matters were put forward in the form of a motion which was open to discussion. In some cases it was done once, in others three times, thus anticipating the practice of Parliament in requiring that a bill be read a third time before it becomes law. If the discussion showed a difference of opinion, it was to be settled by the vote of the majority through balloting.

The Buddhist approach to political power is the moralization and the responsible use of public power. The Buddha preached non-violence and peace as a universal message. He did not approve of violence or the destruction of life, and declared that there is no such thing as a 'just' war. He taught: 'The victor breeds hatred, the defeated lives in misery. He who renounces both victory and defeat is happy and peaceful.' Not only did the Buddha teach non-violence and peace, He was perhaps the first and only religious teacher who went to the battlefield personally to prevent the outbreak of a war. He diffused tension between the Sakyas and the Koliyas who were about to wage war over the waters of Rohini. He also dissuaded King Ajatasattu from attacking the Kingdom of the Vajjis.

The Buddha discussed the importance and the prerequisites of a good government. He showed how the country could become corrupt, degenerate and unhappy when the head of the government becomes corrupt and unjust. He spoke against corruption and how a government should act based on humanitarian principles.

The Buddha once said, 'When the ruler of a country is just and good, the ministers become just and good; when the ministers are just and good, the higher officials become just and good; when the higher officials are just and good, the-rank and file become just and good; when the rank and file become just and good, the people become just and good.'(Anguttara Nikaya)

In the Cakkavatti Sihananda Sutta, the Buddha said that immorality and crime, such as theft, falsehood, violence, hatred, cruelty, could arise from poverty. Kings and governments may try to suppress crime through punishment, but it is futile to eradicate crimes through force.

In the Kutadanta Sutta, the Buddha suggested economic development instead of force to reduce crime. The government should use the country's resources to improve the economic conditions of the country. It could embark on agricultural and rural development, provide financial support to entrepreneurs and business, provide adequate wages for workers to maintain a decent life with human dignity. In the Jataka, the Buddha had given to rules for Good Government, known as 'Dasa Raja Dharma'. These ten rules can be applied even today by any government which wishes to rule the country peacefully. The rules are as follows:

be liberal and avoid selfishness,

maintain a high moral character,

be prepared to sacrifice one's own pleasure for the well-being of the subjects,

be honest and maintain absolute integrity,

be kind and gentle,

lead a simple life for the subjects to emulate,

be free from hatred of any kind,

exercise non-violence,

practise patience, and

respect public opinion to promote peace and harmony.

Regarding the behavior of rulers, He further advised:

A good ruler should act impartially and should not be biased and discriminate between one particular group of subjects against another.

A good ruler should not harbor any form of hatred against any of his subjects.

A good ruler should show no fear whatsoever in the enforcement of the law, if it is justifiable.

A good ruler must possess a clear understanding of the law to be enforced. It should not be enforced just because the ruler has the authority to enforce the law. It must be done in a reasonable manner and with common sense.

(Cakkavatti Sihananda Sutta)

In the Milinda Panha,it is stated: 'If a man, who is unfit, incompetent, immoral, improper, unable and unworthy of kingship, has enthroned himself a king or a ruler with great authority, he is subject to be tortured?to be subject to a variety of punishment by the people, because, being unfit and unworthy, he has placed himself unrighteously in the seat of sovereignty. The ruler, like others who violate and transgress moral codes and basic rules of all social laws of mankind, is equally subject to punishment; and moreover, to be censured is the ruler who conducts himself as a robber of the public.' In a Jataka story, it is mentioned that a ruler who punishes innocent people and does not punish the culprit is not suitable to rule a country.

The king always improves himself and carefully examines his own conduct in deeds, words and thoughts, trying to discover and listen to public opinion as to whether or not he had been guilty of any faults and mistakes in ruling the kingdom. If it is found that he rules unrighteously, the public will complain that they are ruined by the wicked ruler with unjust treatment, punishment, taxation, or other oppressions including corruption of any kind, and they will react against him in one way or another. On the contrary, if he rules righteously they will bless him: 'Long live His Majesty.' (Majjhima Nikaya)

The Buddha'semphasis on the moral duty of a ruler to use public power to improve the welfare of the people had inspired Emperor Asoka in the Third Century B.C. to do likewise. Emperor Asoka, a sparkling example of this principle, resolved to live according to and preach the Dhamma and to serve his subjects and all humanity. He declared his non-aggressive intentions to his neighbors, assuring them of his goodwill and sending envoys to distant kings bearing his message of peace and non-aggression. He promoted the energetic practice of the socio-moral virtues of honesty, truthfulness, compassion, benevolence, non-violence, considerate behavior towards all, non-extravagance, non-acquisitiveness, and non-injury to animals.

He encouraged religious freedom and mutual respect for each other's creed. He went on periodic tours preaching the Dhamma to the rural people. He undertook works of public utility, such as founding of hospitals for men and animals, supplying of medicine, planting of roadside trees and groves, digging of wells, and construction of watering sheds and rest houses. He expressly forbade cruelty to animals.

Sometimes the Buddha is said to be a social reformer. Among other things, He condemned the caste system, recognized the equality of people, spoke on the need to improve socio-economic conditions, recognized the importance of a more equitable distribution of wealth among the rich and the poor, raised the status of women, recommended the incorporation of humanism in government and administration, and taught that a society should not be run by greed but with consideration and compassion for the people.

Despite all these, His contribution to mankind is much greater because He took off at a point which no other social reformer before or ever since had done, that is, by going to the deepest roots of human ill which are found in the human mind. It is only in the human mind that true reform can be effected. Reforms imposed by force upon the external world have a very short life because they have no roots. But those reforms which spring as a result of the transformation of man's inner consciousness remain rooted. While their branches spread outwards, they draw their nourishment from an unfailing source _the subconscious imperatives of the life-stream itself. So reforms come about when men's minds have prepared the way for them, and they live as long as men revitalize them out of their own love of truth, justice and their fellow men.

The doctrine preached by the Buddha is not one based on 'Political Philosophy'. Nor is it a doctrine that encourages men to worldly pleasures. It sets out a way to attain Nibbana. In other words, its ultimate aim is to put an end to craving (Tanha) that keeps them in bondage to this world. A stanza from the Dhammapada best summarizes this statement: 'The path that leads to worldly gain is one, and the path that leads to Nibbana(by leading a religious life)is another.' However, this does not mean that Buddhists cannot or should not get involved in the political process, which is a social reality. The lives of the members of a society are shaped by laws and regulations, economic arrangements allowed within a country, institutional arrangements, which are influenced by the political arrangements of that society., Nevertheless, if a Buddhist wishes to be involved in politics, he should not misuse religion to gain political powers, nor is it advisable for those who have renounced the worldly life to lead a pure, religious life to be actively involved in politics.

7

Buddhist Views on Marriage

In Buddhism, marriage is regarded as entirely a personal, individual concern and not as a religious duty.

Marriage is a social convention, an institution created by man for the well-being and happiness of man, to differentiate human society from animal life and to maintain order and harmony in the process of procreation. Even though the Buddhist texts are silent on the subject of monogamy or polygamy, the Buddhist laity is advised to limit themselves to one wife. The Buddha did not lay rules on married life but gave necessary advice on how to live a happy married life. There are ample inferences in His sermons that it is wise and advisable to be faithful to one wife and not to be sensual and to run after other women. The Buddha realized that one of the main causes of man's downfall is his involvement with other women (Parabhava Sutta).Man must realize the difficulties, the trials and tribulations that he has to undergo just to maintain a wife and a family. These would be magnified many times when faced with calamities. Knowing the frailties of human nature, the Buddha did, in one of His precepts, advise His followers of refrain from committing adultery or sexual misconduct.

The Buddhist views on marriage are very liberal: in Buddhism, marriage is regarded entirely as personal and individual concern, and not as a religious duty. There are no religious laws in Buddhism compelling a person to be married, to remain as a bachelor or to lead a life of total chastity. It is not laid down anywhere that Buddhists must produce children or regulate the number of children that they produce. Buddhism allows each individual the freedom to decide for himself all the issues pertaining to marriage. It might be asked why Buddhist monks do not marry, since there are no laws for or against marriage. The reason is obviously that to be of service to mankind, the monks have chosen a way of life which includes celibacy.

Those who renounce the worldly life keep away from married life voluntarily to avoid various worldly commitments in order to maintain peace of mind and to dedicate their lives solely to serve others in the attainment of spiritual emancipation. Although Buddhist monks do not solemnize a marriage ceremony, they do perform religious services in order to bless the couples.

DIVORCE

Separation or divorce is not prohibited in Buddhism though the necessity would scarcely arise if the Buddha's injunctions were strictly followed. Men and women must have the liberty to separate if they really cannot agree with each other. Separation is preferable to avoid miserable family life for a long period of time. The Buddha further advises old men not to have young wives as the old and young are unlikely to be compatible, which can create undue problems, disharmony and downfall (Parabhava Sutta).

A society grows through a network of relationships which are mutually inter-twined and inter-dependent. Every relationship is a whole hearted commitment to support and to protect others in a group or community. Marriage plays a very important part in this strong web of relationships of giving support and protection. A good marriage should grow and develop gradually from understanding and not impulse, from true loyalty and not just sheer indulgence. The institution of marriage provides a fine basis for the development of culture, a delightful association of two individuals to be nurtured, and to be free from loneliness, deprivation and fear. In marriage, each partner develops a complementary role, giving strength and moral courage to one another, each manifesting a supportive and appreciative recognition of the other's skills. There must be no thought of either man or woman being superior?each is complementary to the other, a partnership of equality, exuding gentleness, generosity, calm and dedication.

BIRTH CONTROL, ABORTION AND SUICIDE

Although man has freedom to plan his family according to his own convenience, abortion is not justifiable.

There is no reason for Buddhists to oppose birth control. They are at liberty to use any of the old or modern measures to prevent conception. Those who object to birth control by saying that it is against God's law to practise it, must realize that their concept regarding this issue is not reasonable. In birth control what is done is to prevent the coming into being of an existence. There is no killing involved and there is no akusala kamma. But if they take any action to have an abortion, this action is wrong because it involves taking away or destroying a visible or invisible life. Therefore, abortion is not justifiable. According to the Teachings of the Buddha, five conditions must be present to constitute the evil act of killing. They are:

a living being

knowledge or awareness it is a living being

intention of killing

effort to kill, and

consequent death

When a female conceives, there is a being in her womb and this fulfills the first condition. After a couple of months, she knows that there is a-new life within her and this satisfies the second condition. Then for some reason or other, she wants to do away with this being in her. So she begins to search for an abortionist to do the job and in this way, the third condition is fulfilled. When the abortionist does his job, the fourth condition is provided for and finally, the being is killed because of that action. So all the conditions are present. In this way, there is a violation of the First Precept 'not to kill', and this is tantamount to killing a human being. According to Buddhism, there is no ground to say that we have the right to take away the life of another.

Under certain circumstances, people feel compelled to do that for their own convenience. But they should not justify this act of abortion as somehow or other they will have to face some sort of bad karmic results. In certain countries abortion is legalized, but this is to overcome some problems. Religious principles should never be surrendered for the pleasure of man. They stand for the welfare of the whole mankind.

Committing Suicide

Taking one's own life under any circumstances is morally and spiritually wrong. Taking one's own life owing to frustration or disappointment only causes greater suffering. Suicide is a cowardly way to end one's problems of life. A person cannot commit suicide if his mind is pure and tranquil. If one leaves this world with a confused and frustrated mind, it is most unlikely that he would be born again in a better condition. Suicide is an unwholesome or unskillful act since it is encouraged by a mind filled with greed, hatred and delusion. Those who commit suicide have not learnt how to face their problems, how to face the facts of life, and how to use their mind in a proper manner. Such people have not been able to understand the nature of life and worldly conditions.

Some people sacrifice their own lives for what they deem as a good and noble cause. They take their own life by such methods as self-immolation, bullet-fire, or starvation. Such actions may be classified as brave and courageous. However, from the Buddhist point of view, such acts are not to be condoned. The Buddha has clearly pointed out that the suicidal states of mind lead to further suffering.

There is really no ground to think that this is the only period in which the population of the world has increased.

If Buddhists do not believe in the soul created by god, how are they going to account for the increase of population in the world today? This is a very common question that is asked by many people today. People who ask this question usually assume that there is only one world where living beings exist. One must consider that it is quite natural for the population to increase in such places where good climatic conditions, medical facilities, food and precautions are available to produce and to protect living beings.

One must also consider that there is really no ground to think that this is the only period in which the population in the world has increased. There are no means of comparison with any period of ancient history. Vast civilizations existed and have disappeared in Central Asia, the Middle East, Africa and Ancient America. No census figures on these civilizations are even remotely available. Population, as everything else in the universe, is subject to cycles of rise and fall. In cycles of alarming increases of birth rate, one might be consequently tempted to argue against rebirth in this or other worlds.

For the last few thousand years, there has been no evidence to prove that there were more people in some parts of the world than there are today. The number of beings existing in the various world systems is truly infinite. If human lives can be compared to only one grain of sand, the number of beings in the universe is like the grains of sand all the beaches in the world. When conditions are right and when supported by their good kamma, a few of these infinite number of beings are reborn as human beings. The advancement of medicine especially in the 19th and 20th centuries has enabled human beings to live longer and healthier lives.

This is a factor that contributes to population increase. Population can further increase unless sensible people take measures to control it. Hence, the credit or responsibility of increasing the population must be given to medical facilities and other circumstances available today. This credit or responsibility cannot be allotted to any particular religion or any external sources.

There is a belief among certain people that all unfortunate occurrences that destroy human lives are created by god in order to reduce the population of the world. Instead of giving so much suffering to his own creatures, why cannot he control the population? Why does he create more and more people in thickly populated countries where there is no proper food, clothing and other basic and necessary requirements? Those who believe that god created everything cannot give a satisfactory answer to this question. Poverty, unhappiness, war, hunger, disease, famine are not due to the will of god or to the whim of some devil, but to causes which are not so difficult to discover.

SEX AND RELIGION

'The lower part of us is still animal.'(Gandhi)

The sex impulse is the most dynamic force in human nature. So far-reaching is the sexual force that some measures of self-control is necessary even in ordinary existence. In the case of the spiritual aspirant, for whoever wants to bring his mind under complete control, a still greater measure of self-discipline is necessary. Such a powerful force in human character can be subdued only if the aspirant controls his thoughts and practises concentration. The conservation of the sexual force helps to develop this strength. For if he controls the sexual force, he will have more control over his whole make-up, over his lesser emotions.

Celibacy is one of the requirements for those who like to develop their spiritual development to perfection. However, it is not compulsory for each and every person to observe complete celibacy in order to practise Buddhism. The Buddha's advice is that observing celibacy is more congenial for a person who wants to cultivate his spiritual achievements. For ordinary Buddhist laymen, the precept is to abstain from sexual misconduct. Although perversion of the sexual force is not under this same category, the perverted person invariably suffers bad reactions either physically, or mentally or both.

There is a need for Buddhist laymen to exercise some degree of control over their sexual force. Man's sexual urge must be controlled properly otherwise man will behave worse than an animal when he is intoxicated with lust. Consider the sexual behavior of what we call the 'lower animal'. Which really is often 'lower'? The animal or the man? Which acts in a normal, regular manner as regards sexual behavior? And which runs off into all manner of irregularities and perversities? Often it is the animal that is the higher creature and man that is the lower. And why is this? It is simply because man who possesses the mental capacity which if rightly used, could make him master over his sex impulses, has actually used his mental powers in such deplorable fashion as to make himself more a slave to those impulses. Thus man can, at times, be considered lower than the animal.

Our ancestors played down this sexual impulse; they knew that it was strong enough without giving it any extra encouragement. But today we have blown it up with a thousand forms of incitation, suggestive advertisements, emphasis and display; and we have armed the sexual force with the doctrine that inhibition is dangerous and can even cause mental disorders.

Yet inhibition the control of impulse is the first principle of any civilization. In our modern civilization, we have polluted the sexual atmosphere that surrounds us. So great is the mind-body urge for sexual gratification.

As a result of this sex exploitation by the hidden persuaders of modern society, the youth of today have developed an attitude toward sex that is becoming a public nuisance. An innocent girl has no freedom to move anywhere without being disturbed. On the other hand, females should be dressed such a manner as not to arouse the hidden animal nature of youths.

Man is the only animal that does not have periods of natural sexual inactivity during which the body can recover its vitality. Unfortunately, commercial exploitation of the erotic nature in man has caused modern man to be exposed to a ceaseless barrage of sexual stimulation from every side. Much of the neuroses of present-day life is traceable to this unbalanced state of affairs. Men are expected to be monogamous, yet women are encouraged in every possible way to 'glamorize' themselves, not for the husband alone, but to excite in every man passions that society forbids him to indulge in.

Many societies try to enforce monogamous relationships. Thus a man with many failings can still be a moral man, meaning that he is faithful to the one wife that the law allows him to have. The danger here lies in the fact that thoughtful people who are intelligent enough to realize that these rules are artificial and not based on any transcendental, universally valid principles, are liable to fall into the error of thinking the same about all the other ethical laws.

Sex should be given its due place in normal human life; it should be neither unhealthily repressed nor morbidly exaggerated. And it should always be under the control of the will, as it can be if it is regarded sanely and placed in its proper perspective.

Sex should not be considered as the most important ingredient for one's happiness in a married life. Those who over-indulge can become slaves to sex which would ultimately ruin love and humane consideration in marriage. As in everything, one must be temperate and rational in one's sexual demands taking into consideration one another's intimate feelings and temperament.

Marriage is a bond of partnership for life entered into by a man and a woman. Patience, tolerance and understanding are the three principal qualities that should be developed and nurtured by the couple. Whilst love should be the knot tying the couple together, material necessities for sustaining a happy home should be made available by the male partner for the couple to share. The qualification for a good partnership in marriage should be 'ours' and not 'yours' or 'mine' . A good couple should 'open' their hearts to one another and to refrain from entertaining 'secrets'. Keeping secrets to oneself could lead to suspicion and suspicion is the element that could destroy love in a partnership. Suspicion breeds jealousy, jealousy creates anger, anger develops hatred, hatred turns into enmity and enmity could cause untold suffering including bloodshed, suicide and even murder.

DOES BUDDHISM TREAT WOMEN AS SECOND-CLASS CITIZENS?

India is a patriarchal society. Even amongst the wider ex-untouchable Buddhist community the women are often discriminated against, even in their own homes. However, Indian women involved in TBMSG are not discriminated against within the Movement. If they choose, they can study and practice Buddhism at the same intensity as their male counterparts. Not restricted by gender-based divisions they can meditate, attend retreats, practice the same five or ten precepts, earn their livelihood, become mitras and Dharmacharinis in likewise manner to the men. They are neither seen as inferior nor subservient to the male mitras and Dharmacharis. Such a radical change and breakthrough is one that was strongly encouraged by Dr Ambedkar.

In 1950, six years before the mass conversions to Buddhism of the ex- Untouchables under the leadership of Dr B.R. Ambedkar, an article appeared in Eves Weekly, an Indian women's popular magazine, entitled Our New Republic, in which the Hindu author made the following two statements: 1. It was alas the Buddhist theory that seems to have thrust women into the background. 2. The Buddha was ever exhorting men to beware of women.

In an article in the MahaBodhi Journal, Lama Govinda challenged and refuted both statements. Dr Ambedkar went further. Feeling so strongly about these charges leveled against the Buddha, he examined the question and wrote an article entitled The Rise and Fall of Hindu Woman. Who was Responsible for it? In this article he maintained that the decline and fall of Indian women should be attributed to Manu, the lawgiver of the Hindus, and not to the Buddha. Ambedkar felt the above charges could be supported on two grounds only. Firstly he refers to the Mahaparanibbana Sutta of the Sutta Pitaka, Chapter 5, which reads:

How are we to conduct ourselves (asks Ananda) with regard to womankind? As not seeing them Ananda, (replies the Buddha.) But if we should see them, what are we to do? Not talking Ananda. But if they should speak to us Lord, what are we to do? Keep wide-awake Ananda.

Dr Ambedkar examined this passage to determine whether or not it was original and genuine, or a later interpolation of the bhikkhus. The Sutta Pitaka as we find it now is, according to Dr Ambedkar: Wrapped about by mythical drapery, disfigured by additions of purely Brahman ideas entirely foreign to the original Buddhist thought, and distorted by twists and turns given to it by monastic ideas intended to enforce monastic ideals.

The Sutta Pitaka was not written until four hundred years after the Buddhas Parinirvana. Ambedkar suggests that since the editors were monks, they compiled and wrote for the monk. In this way the Buddhas statement was seen as being valuable for the monk in order to preserve his rule of celibacy. Ambedkar also supported his suggestion by noting that many passages occurring in this Sutta also occur in other Suttas, whereas this particular passage does not. There is moreover also a Chinese version of the Sutta, which does not contain this passage.

The Buddha's and Ananda's attitude to women as reported generally in the Pitakas seems contrary to the Buddhas answer to Anandas question in this instance. For example, in the very same Sutta, the Buddha describes the wonderful qualities of Ananda, including the following:

If, Brethren, a number of the sisters of the Order . . . or devout women should behold him, and if Ananda should preach the truth to them, they are filled with joy at the discourse; while the company is ill at ease, Brethren, when Ananda is silent. Both the Buddha and Ananda met and discoursed with women. It therefore seems unlikely, according to Ambedkar, that such a question would have been asked. Personally, I think it may have been asked, but as a general question, and perhaps it was good adviee to most monks!

Ambedkar thought the second support for the charges against the Buddha was the so called subordination of the bhikshuni Sangha to the Bhikkhu proof in the Pali suttas that the Buddha did not regard women as inferior to men either in point of intellect, character, or spiritual attainments-as when Ananda asked the Buddha:

Lord, are women capable, after Going Forth from the house life into homelessness in the Law and Discipline declared by the Perfect One, of realizing the fruit of Stream Entry or Once-Return or Non-Return or Arahantship? They are Ananda!

Presumably, had he feared that their presence in the order might lower the prestige of the Sangha, he would never have admitted them. He chose, according to Ambedkar, to have two separate sanghas for fear that co-fraternity of men and women who had left home and become monks and nuns would soon weaken and probably break the rule of celibacy. The Buddha promoted the view that it is the sex instinct, which drives a man into woman's bondage, and a woman into mans. The bhikkhus were the ones already instructed in the Buddhas doctrine, whereas the women had not yet been instructed. The women would therefore have to be under the instruction of the men. Ambedkar felt this to be a simple practical matter, and not one of the subordination of the women to the authority of the men.

Under Hindu Brahman theory-and contrary to Buddhism-women are denied the right to acquire knowledge, or even the right to study the Vedic scriptures. It is stated in the Mane Smrti, the sacred law book of the Hindus which even today still gives scriptural authority for the inhuman treatment of the (officially ex-) Untouchables, that: Women have no right to study the Vedas, that is why their rites are performed without Vedic mantras. Women have- no knowledge of religion because they have no right to know the Vedas. The uttering of Vedic mantras is useful for removing sin. As women cannot utter the Vedic mantras they are as Untruth is.

The freedom enjoyed by Buddhist women being allowed and able to realize their spiritual potential was so great that bhikshuni Mettika, a Brahmin woman by birth, sang out aloud: So sit I here upon this rock, and oer my spirit sweeps the breath of Liberty. To gain this freedom the bhikshunis had given up social position and domestic success. Even in India today this is still highly prized for women, yet it cramps, stultifies, and binds them to the home, making the possibility of their stepping out as individuals virtually impossible. There was a time, before Manu, when women could rise high in learning and education, and when women were highly respected. It was Manu, according to Ambedkar, the lawgiver of the Hindus, feeling threatened woman's downfall. Knowing that the home was the place to be protected against Buddhism, it was the women in particular whom he put under restraint.

The mere fact the Ambedkar chose to write this article on women, using relevant quotations from the Buddhist scriptures, indicates that he recognized the spiritual potential even spiritual realization, of women Buddhists. His writings and speeches on Buddhism were addressed to both men and women. When speaking on Buddhism as A Perfect Religion he talks about equality: Equality not just between man and man only, but between man and woman. Like the Buddha, Ambedkar spoke not only to half the human race, but also to men and women. Uninspired by the Bhikkhu Sangha in 11 India, which seemed to place far more emphasis on monastic status than sincere practice,

Ambedkar felt, at the time of the mass conversions, that a new Buddhist movement was needed, a Sangha which did not depend on the bhikkhus, a Sangha in which there would be no discrimination of caste, class, colour, or gender. TBMSG is fulfilling his wish in the sense of being a Sangha consisting of men and women primarily committed to Going for Refuge to the Three Jewels, without discrimination. It is for this reason that TBMSG has been so successful in being the life force behind the Dharma Revolution in India. The women of TBMSG play a large part in this revival of Buddhism, and I have witnessed quite dramatic changes in many of their lives.

One such woman is Dharmacharini Vimalashuri. She was born an Untouchable. Through the encouragement of Dr Ambedkar she gained an education. This enabled her to see through her caste and gender discrimination. Eventually after much searching she discovered TBMSG. Now she is able to practice and teach the Dharma freely.

She is someone who, under the influence of Dr Ambedkar's views and now TBMSG, has changed enormously. She along with others is a great inspiration to other women Buddhists.

8

Discourses of the Ancient Nuns

INTRODUCTION

The growing interest in women's spirituality has led to a renewed focus upon the Therigatha, the Verses of the Elder Nuns, as the oldest existing testament to the feminine experience of Buddhism. Despite this recent attention to the Therigatha, however, it seems that all but a few scholarly commentators have overlooked a short chapter in the Samyutta Nikaya that serves as an important supplement to the larger work. This is the Bhikkhuni-samyutta, Chapter 5 of the Sagathavagga-samyutta, the Connected Discourses with Verses, Volume I of the Samyutta Nikaya.

The Bhikkhuni-samyutta is a compilation of ten short suttas in mixed prose and verse, with a total of thirty-seven verses. Though several of these verses have parallels in the Therigatha (mentioned in the notes), a significant number don't, and often the variations in roughly parallel versions are themselves of intrinsic interest.

At least one nun in the Bhikkhuni-samyutta, Vajira, does not appear in the Therigatha, while the case of another nun, Sela, is problematic. A comparison between the two collections also brings to light some noteworthy differences in the ascription of authorship; in one case -- that of the three Cala sisters-- a three-way shuffling of ascriptions occurs. Such differences can be readily understood once we realize that the texts were originally transmitted orally for several centuries and thus were contingent on less durable factors than paper and ink.

Since the Samyutta Nikaya and the Therigatha were evidently transmitted by different lines of reciters, it was only too easy for verses to break off from their original narrative setting and merge with a different background story connecting them to a different author.

The antiquity of this collection is attested to by the fact that it has a counterpart in the Chinese translation of the Sanskrit Samyuktagama, which probably belonged to the Sarvastivada school. Anesaki's The Four Buddhist Agamas in Chinese gives a breakdown of the Chinese equivalent of the Bhikkhuni-samyutta, and though the order of suttas is different, the ten titles are almost identical, except that the Pali Sela Sutta is there entitled Viri (or Vira). This is strong evidence that the entire chapter had taken shape before the Pali and Sarvastivada schools went their separate ways.

All the ten suttas are constructed according to the same pattern, a direct confrontation between Mara the Evil One, the Lord of Sensuality, and an individual nun. This structure perhaps accounts for the placement of the Bhikkhuni-samyutta immediately after the Mara-samyutta, in which the Evil One is shown trying to distract the Buddha and the monks. In each sutta of our collection a nun goes off by herself to pass the day in solitary meditation. Then Mara approaches her with a challenge -- a provocative question or a taunt -- intending to make her fall away from concentration. What Mara has failed to realize is that each of these nuns is an arahant and has seen so deeply into the truth of the Dhamma that she is utterly inaccessible to his wiles. Far from being flustered by Mara's challenge, the nun promptly guesses the identity of her adversary and overturns his challenge with a sharp reply. Once Mara realizes that his number has been called he has no choice but to vanish on the spot, "sad and disappointed."

In a dialogue that brings together the Lord of Sensuality with a solitary nun one might expect each of Mara's overtures to be aimed at sexual seduction. This, however, is so only in several suttas. The actual themes of the discourses vary and expose us to a broad range of perspectives on the attitudes and insights of the renunciant life. The contrast between the allurement and misery of sensual pleasures is the theme of §§ 1, 4, and 5. In §1, Mara does not himself attempt to seduce the nun but only urges her to enjoy sense pleasures before her time runs out; in §4 he assumes the guise of a handsome youth who lavishes his seductive charms on the beautiful Vijaya; and in §5 he almost threatens to rape the nun Uppalavanna, who had actually been raped soon after her ordination by an infatuated youth. In all three cases the nuns sharply rebuke Mara with verses that reveal their utter indifference to his solicitations.

In §3, Mara approaches Kisagotami, the heroine of the well-known parable of the mustard seed, trying to arouse her maternal instincts to beget another son. His challenge thus touches on sensuality only indirectly. His primary appeal is aimed at awakening the feminine desire for children.

Mara's dialogue with Soma (§2) voices the ancient Indian prejudice that women are endowed with "mere two-fingered wisdom" (an obscure expression that tries the ingenuity of the commentators), and thus cannot attain Nibbana, a goal reserved for males. Soma's rejoinder is a forceful reminder that enlightenment does not depend on gender but on the mind's capacity for concentration and wisdom, qualities accessible to any human being who earnestly seeks to penetrate the truth.

In §§6, 7, and 8 we meet the three Cala sisters, the younger sisters of the Venerable Sariputta. From these three nuns Mara tries to elicit, respectively, an affirmation of birth (i.e. of life in general), of rebirth in the heavenly realms, and of heretical views. In each case the nun replies with appropriate verses exposing the dangers in birth, in the entire triple world, and in the systems of the non-Buddhist thinkers.

The last two suttas are philosophical masterpieces, compressing into a few tight stanzas insights of enormous depth and wide implications. Full appreciation of their richness and power would require extensive acquaintance with the whole corpus of early Buddhist texts, particularly the Samyutta Nikaya chapters on dependent origination (No. 12) and the five aggregates (No. 22). In §9, Mara challenges Sela with a question on the origins of personal existence. She replies with a masterly poem that condenses the whole teaching of dependent origination into three four-line stanzas, adorned with an illuminating simile. In §10 he poses a similar problem to Vajira, who answers with a stunning exposition of the teaching of non-self, illustrating the composite nature of personal identity with the simile of the chariot. This simile was popularized by the famous Milindapañha, but Vajira's simpler version has an incisive edge that is blunted by the bombastic tone of the later work.

Though set against a mythological background in an ancient world whose customs and norms seem so remote from our own, these poems of the nuns of old still speak to us today through their sheer simplicity and uncompromising honesty. They need no ornamentation or artifice to convey their message but startle us with the clarity of unadorned truth. Emerging from the depths of indubitable personal realization, crackling with insight, they point unwaveringly towards the rugged path of renunciation and wisdom that leads to the end of suffering.

The present translation is based primarily upon the Burmese script Chatthasangayana edition of the Samyutta Nikaya (Be), though I also consulted the Sinhala script Buddha Jayanti edition (Ce) and the PTS's Roman script edition (Ee). Numbers in square brackets are the page numbers of the PTS edition.

BHIKKHUNI-SAMYUTTA

Alavika

Thus have I heard. On one occasion the Blessed One was dwelling at Savatthi in Jeta's Grove, Anathapindika's Park.

Then, in the morning, the bhikkhuni Alavika dressed and, taking bowl and robe, entered Savatthi for alms. When she had walked for alms in Savatthi and had returned from her alms round, after her meal she went to the Blind Men's Grove seeking seclusion. Then Mara the Evil One, desiring to arouse fear, trepidation, and terror in the bhikkhuni Alavika, desiring to make her fall away from seclusion, approached her and addressed her in verse:

"There is no escape in the world,

So what will you do with seclusion?

Enjoy the delights of sensual pleasure:

Don't be remorseful later!"

Then it occurred to the bhikkhuni Alavika: "Now who is it that recited the verse -- a human being or a non-human being?" Then it occurred to her: "This is Mara the Evil One, who has recited the verse desiring to arouse fear, trepidation, and terror in me, desiring to make me fall away from seclusion."

Then the bhikkhuni Alavika, having understood, "This is Mara the Evil One," replied to him in verses:

"There is an escape in the world
Which I have closely touched with wisdom.
O Evil One, kinsman of the negligent,
You do not know that state.

Sensual pleasures are like sword stakes;
The aggregates, their chopping block.
What you call sensual delight
Has become for me non-delight."

Then Mara the Evil One, realizing, "The bhikkhuni Alavika knows me," sad and disappointed, disappeared right there.

Soma

Setting at Savatthi. Then, in the morning, the bhikkhuni Soma dressed and, taking bowl and robe, entered Savatthi for alms. When she had walked for alms in Savatthi and had returned from her alms round, after her meal she went to the Blind Men's Grove for the day's abiding. Having plunged into the Blind Men's Grove, she sat down at the foot of a tree for the day's abiding.

Then Mara the Evil One, desiring to arouse fear, trepidation, and terror in the bhikkhuni Soma, desiring to make her fall away from concentration, approached her and addressed her in verse:

"That state so hard to achieve
Which is to be attained by the seers,
Can't be attained by a woman
With her two-fingered wisdom."

Then it occurred to the bhikkhuni Soma: "Now who is this that recited the verse -- a human being or a non-human being?" Then it occurred to her: "This is Mara the Evil One, who has recited the verse desiring to arouse fear, trepidation, and terror in me, desiring to make me fall away from concentration."

Then the bhikkhuni Soma, having understood, "This is Mara the Evil One," replied to him in verses:

"What does womanhood matter at all
When the mind is concentrated well,
When knowledge flows on steadily
As one sees correctly into Dhamma.

One to whom it might occur,
'I'm a woman' or 'I'm a man'
Or 'I'm anything at all' --
Is fit for Mara to address."

Then Mara the Evil One, realizing, "The bhikkhuni Soma knows me," sad and disappointed, disappeared right there.

Gotami

Setting at Savatthi. Then, in the morning, the bhikkhuni Kisagotami dressed and, taking bowl and robe, entered Savatthi for alms. When she had walked for alms in Savatthi and had returned from her alms round, after her meal she went to the Blind Men's Grove for the day's abiding. Having plunged into the Blind Men's Grove, she sat down at the foot of a tree for the day's abiding.

Then Mara the Evil One, desiring to arouse fear, trepidation, and terror in the bhikkhuni Kisagotami, desiring to make her fall away from concentration, approached her and addressed her in verse:

"Why now, when your son is dead,

Do you sit alone with tearful face?

Having entered the woods all alone,

Are you on the lookout for a man?"

Then it occurred to the bhikkhuni Kisagotami: "Now who is this that recited the verse -- a human being or a non-human being?" Then it occurred to her: "This is Mara the Evil One, who has recited the verse desiring to arouse fear, trepidation, and terror in me, desiring to make me fall away from concentration."

Then the bhikkhuni Kisagotami, having understood, "This is Mara the Evil One," replied to him in verses:

"I've gotten past the death of sons;

With this, the search for men has ended.

I do not sorrow, I do not weep,

Nor do I fear you, friend.

Delight everywhere has been destroyed,

The mass of darkness has been sundered.

Having conquered the army of Death,

I dwell without defiling taints."

Then Mara the Evil One, realizing, "The bhikkhuni Kisagotami knows me," sad and disappointed, disappeared right there.

Vijaya

Setting at Savatthi. Then, in the morning, the bhikkhuni Vijaya dressed ... she sat down at the foot of a tree for the day's abiding. Then Mara the Evil One, desiring to arouse fear, trepidation, and terror in the bhikkhuni Vijaya, desiring to make her fall away from concentration, approached her and addressed her in verse:

"You are so young and beautiful,

And I too am in the bloom of youth.

Come, noble lady, let us rejoice

With the music of a fivefold ensemble."

Then it occurred to the bhikkhuni Vijaya: "Now who is this...? This is Mara the Evil One ... desiring to make me fall away from concentration."

Then the bhikkhuni Vijaya, having understood, "This is Mara the Evil One," replied to him in verses:

"Forms and sounds, tastes and odours,

Tactile objects that delight the mind:

I offer them right back to you,

For I, O Mara, do not need them.

I am repelled and humiliated

By this foul, putrid body,

Subject to break up, fragile:

I've uprooted sensual craving.

As to those beings who fare amidst form,

And those who abide in the formless,

And those peaceful attainments too:

Everywhere darkness has been destroyed."

Then Mara the Evil One, realizing "The bhikkhuni Vijaya knows me," sad and disappointed, disappeared right there.

Uppalavanna

Setting at Savatthi. Then, in the morning, the bhikkhuni Uppalavanna dressed ... she stood at the foot of a sala tree in full flower. Then Mara the Evil One, desiring to arouse fear, trepidation, and terror in the bhikkhuni Uppalavanna, desiring to make her fall away from concentration, approached her and addressed her in verse:

"Having gone to a sala tree with flowering top,
You stand at its foot all alone, bhikkhuni.
There is none whose beauty can rival your own:
Foolish girl, have you no fear of rogues?"

Then it occurred to the bhikkhuni Uppalavanna: "Now who is this...? This is Mara the Evil One ... desiring to make me fall away from concentration."

Then the bhikkhuni Uppalavanna, having understood, "This is Mara the Evil One," replied to him in verses:

"Though a hundred thousand rogues
Just like you might come here,
I stir not a hair, I feel no terror;
Even alone, Mara, I don't fear you.

I can make myself disappear
Or I can enter inside your belly.
I can stand between your eyebrows
Yet you won't catch a glimpse of me.

I am the master of my own mind,
The bases of power are well developed;
I am freed from every kind of bondage,
Therefore I don't fear you, friend."

Then Mara the Evil One, realizing, "The bhikkhuni Uppalavanna knows me," sad and disappointed, disappeared right there.

Cala

Setting at Savatthi. Then, in the morning, the bhikkhuni Cala dressed ... she sat down at the foot of a tree for the day's abiding.

Then Mara the Evil One approached the bhikkhuni Cala and said to her: "What don't you approve of, bhikkhuni?"

"I don't approve of birth, friend."

"Why don't you approve of birth?
Once born, one enjoys sensual pleasures.
Who now has persuaded you of this:
'Bhikkhuni, don't approve of birth'?"

"For one who is born there is death;
Once born, one encounters sufferings --
Bondage, murder, affliction --
Hence one shouldn't apprcve of birth.

The Buddha has taught the Dhamma,
The transcendence of birth;
For the abandoning of all suffering
He has settled me in the truth.

As to those beings who fare amidst form,
And those who abide in the formless --
Not having understood cessation,
They come again to re-becoming."

Then Mara the Evil One, realizing, "The bhikkhuni Cala knows me," sad and disappointed, disappeared right there.

Upacala

Setting at Savatthi. Then, in the morning, the bhikkhuni Upacala dressed ... she sat down at the foot of a tree for the day's abiding.

Then Mara the Evil One approached the bhikkhuni Upacala and said to her:

"Where do you wish to be reborn, bhikkhuni?"

"I do not wish to be reborn anywhere, friend."

"There are Tavatimsa and Yama devas,
And devatas of the Tusita realm,
Devas who take delight in creating,
And devas who exercise control.
Direct your mind there
And you'll experience delight."[20]

"There are Tavatimsa and Yama devas,
And devatas of the Tusita realm,
Devas who take delight in creating,
And devas who exercise control.
They are still bound by sensual bondage,
They come again under Mara's control.
All the world is on fire,
All the world is burning,
All the world is ablaze,
All the world is quaking.

That which does not quake or blaze,
That to which worldlings do not resort,
Where there is no place for Mara:
That is where my mind delights."

Then Mara the Evil One, realizing, "The bhikkhuni Upacala knows me," sad and disappointed, disappeared right there.

Sisupacala

Setting at Savatthi. Then, in the morning, the bhikkhuni Sisupacala dressed ... she sat down at the foot of a tree for the day's abiding.

Then Mara the Evil One approached the bhikkhuni Sisupacala and said to her: "Whose creed do you approve of, bhikkhuni?"

"I don't approve of anyone's creed, friend."

"Under whom have you shaved your head?
You do appear to be a recluse,
Yet you don't approve of any creed,
So why wander as if bewildered?"[21]

"Outside here the followers of creeds
Place their confidence in views.
I don't approve of their teachings;
They are not skilled in the Dhamma. [134]

But there is a scion of the Sakyan clan,
The Enlightened One, without an equal,
Conqueror of all, Mara's subduer,
Who everywhere is undefeated.

Everywhere freed and unattached,
The One with Vision who sees all,
Who attained the end of all kamma,
Released in the extinction of acquisitions:
That Blessed One is my Teacher;
His is the teaching I approve."

Then Mara the Evil One, realizing, "The bhikkhuni Sisupacala knows me," sad and disappointed, disappeared right there.

Sela

Setting at Savatthi. Then, in the morning, the bhikkhuni Sela dressed ... she sat down at the foot of a tree for the day's abiding.

Then Mara the Evil One, desiring to arouse fear, trepidation, and terror in the bhikkhuni Sela, desiring to make her fall away from concentration, approached her and addressed her in verse:

"By whom has this puppet been created?
Where is the maker of the puppet?
Where has the puppet arisen?
Where does the puppet cease?"

Then it occurred to the bhikkhuni Sela: "Now who is this...? This is Mara the Evil One ... desiring to make me fall away from concentration."

Then the bhikkhuni Sela, having understood, "This is Mara the Evil One," replied to him in verses:

"This puppet is not made by itself,
Nor is this misery made by another.
It has come to be dependent on a cause,
When the cause dissolves then it will cease.

As when a seed is sown in a field
It grows depending on a pair of factors:
It requires both the soil's nutrients
And a steady supply of moisture.

Just so the aggregates and elements,
And these six bases of sensory contact,
Have come to be dependent on a cause;
When the cause dissolves they will cease."

Then Mara the Evil One, realizing, "The bhikkhuni Sela knows me," sad and disappointed, disappeared right there.

Vajira

Setting at Savatthi. Then, in the morning, the bhikkhuni Vajira dressed and, taking bowl and robe, entered Savatthi for alms. When she had walked for alms in Savatthi and had returned from her alms round, after her meal she went to the Blind Men's Grove for the day's abiding. Having plunged into the Blind Men's Grove, she sat down at the foot of a tree for the day's abiding.

Then Mara the Evil One, desiring to arouse fear, trepidation, and terror in the bhikkhuni Vajira, desiring to make her fall away from concentration, approached her and addressed her in verse:

"By whom has this being been created?
Where is the maker of the being?
Where has the being arisen?
Where does the being cease?"

Then it occurred to the bhikkhuni Vajira: "Now who is this that recited the verse -- a human being or a non-human being?" Then it occurred to her: "This is Mara the Evil One, who has recited the verse desiring to arouse fear, trepidation, and terror in me, desiring to make me fall away from concentration."

Then the bhikkhuni Vajira, having understood, "This is Mara the Evil One," replied to him in verses:

"Why now do you assume 'a being'?
Mara, have you grasped a view?
This is a heap of sheer constructions:
Here no being is found.

Just as, with an assemblage of parts,
The word 'chariot' is used,
So, when the aggregates are present,
There's the convention 'a being.'

It's only suffering that comes to be,
Suffering that stands and falls away.
Nothing but suffering comes to be,
Nothing but suffering ceases."

Then Mara the Evil One, realizing, "The bhikkhuni Vajira knows me," sad and disappointed, disappeared right there.

BUDDHIST WOMEN

An account of some famous women who figure prominently in the early Buddhist texts is given in the following pages. The account will show that women were not a negligible factor in the ancient Buddhist community of India.

Abhirupananda was the daughter of a Sakya noble named Khemaka. She was called Nanda the Fair for her great beauty and amiability. Her beloved kinsman, Carabhuta, died on the day on which she was to choose him from amongst her suitors. She had to leave the world against her will. Though she entered the order, she could not forget that she was beautiful. Fearing that, the Buddha would rebuke her, she used to avoid his presence. The Buddha knew that the time had come for her to acquire knowledge and asked Mahapajapati Gotami to bring all the bhikkhunis before him to receive instruction. Nanda sent a proxy for her. The Buddha said, "Let no one come by proxy." So she was compelled to come to him. The Buddha by his supernatural power conjured up a beautiful woman, who became transformed into an old and fading figure. If had the desired effect, and Abhirupananda became an arhat.

Jenti or Jenta was born in a princely family of the Licchavis at Vaisali. She won arhatship after hearing the dhamma preached by the Buddha. She developed the seven Sambojjhangas.

Citta was born at Rajagaha in the family of a leading burgess. When she was of age, she one day heard the master preach and believed in his doctrine. She was ordained by Mahapajapati the Gotami. In her old age she climbed the vulture's peak and lived like a recluse. Her insight expanded and she won arhatship.

Sukka was born at Rajagaha in the family of a rich householder. When she attained years of discretion, she believed in the Master's teaching and became a lay disciple. One day she heard Dhammadinna preach and was so greatly moved that she renounced the world and followed Dhammadinna. She performed all the exercises for acquiring insight and very soon attained arhatship with patisambhida. Thereupon she became a great preacher and was attended by 500 bhikkhus. One day, along with the other bhikkhunis, she went to the hermitage of the bhikkhunis and taught the

Buddha's doctrine in such a way that everybody listened to her with rapt attention; even the tree-spirit was so much moved that it began to praise her. At this the people were excited and came to the sister and listened attentively.

Sela was born in the kingdom of Alavi, as the king's daughter. She was also known as Alavika. One day, while yet a maid, she went with the king and heard the Master preach. She became a believer and lay disciple. A few days after, she took orders and performed the exercises for insight. She subjugated the complexities of thought, word and deed and soon won arhatship. Thereafter she lived at Savatthi when the Buddha was there. She entered Andhavana to meditate after finishing her midday meal. Mara once tried in vain to persuade her to choose the sensuous life.

Siha was born at Vesali as the daughter of General Siha's sister. She was named after her maternal uncle. When she grew up, she heard the Master teaching the Norm to her maternal uncle and became a believer. She was permitted by her parents to enter the order. For seven years she could not acquire insight as her mind became always inclined to objects of external charm. Then she intended to die. She took a noose, hung it round the bough of a tree and fastened it round her neck. Thus she succeeded in impelling her mind to insight which grew within and she won arhatahip. She then took off the rope from her neck and went back to her hermitage.

Sundari Nanda was born in the royal family of the Sakyas. She was known as the beautiful Nanda. Thinking about the fact that her elder brother, her mother, her brother, her sister and her nephew had renounced the world, she too left it. Even after her renunciation, she was obsessed with the idea of her beauty and would not approach the Lord lest she should ber eproached for her folly. The Lord taught her in the same way as he did in the case of Nanda the Fair. She listened to the Master's teaching and enjoyed the benefit of the fruition of the first stage of sanctification. He then instructed her saying, "Nanda, there is in this body not even the smallest essence. It is but a heap of bones covered with flesh and besmeared with blood under the shadow of decay and death." Afterwards she became an arhat.

Khema was born in the royal family of Sagala. She was very beautiful and her skin was like gold. She became the consort of Bimbisara. One day she heard that the Buddha was in the habit of speaking ill of beauty, since then she did not appear before the Buddha. The king was a chief supporter of the Buddha. He asked his court-poets to compose a song on the glories of the Veluvana hermitage and to sing the song very loudly so that the queen might hear it. The royal order was carried out. Khema heard of the beauty of the hermitage and with the king's consent she came to the Veluvana Vihara, where the Buddha was staying at that time.

When she was led before the Buddha, the latter conjured up a woman to be celestial nymph who stood fanning him with a palm leaf. Khema observed this woman like a more beautiful than she and was ashamed of her own grace. Sometime after she noticed again that the woman was passing from youth to middle age and then to old age, till with broken teeth, grey hair, and wrinkled skin, she fell on earth with her palm leaf. Then thought Khema that her beautiful body would meet with the same fate as that of the nymph. Then the Master, who knew her thoughts, said that persons subject to lust suffer from the result of their action, while those freed from all bondage forsake the world.

When the Master had finished speaking, Khema, according to the commentary, attained arhatship and according to the Apadana, she was established in the fruition of the first stage of sanctification and with the king's permission she entered the order before she became an arhat. Thereafter she made a name for her insight and was ranked foremost amongst the bhikkhunis possessing great wisdom. In vain Mara tried to tempt her with sensuous ideas.

Anopama was the daughter of a banker named Majjha living in Saketa. She was of unique beauty. She was sued by many sons of bankers, higher officers of the State, but she thought that there was no happiness in household life. She went to the Master and heard his teachings. Her intelligence matured. She strove hard for insight and was established in the third fruition. On the seventh day thereafter she attained arhatship.

Rohini was born at Vesali in the house of a very prosperous Brahman. When grown up she went to the Master and heard him preach the doctrine. She obtained sotapattiphalam. She converted her parents to Buddha's faith and got permission from them and entered the order. She performed the exercises for acquiring insight and very soon attained arhatship.

Subha was the daughter of a certain goldsmith of Rajagaha. She was very beautiful and was therefore called Subha. When grown up she saw the Master and believed in his doctrine. The Master saw the maturity of her moral faculties and taught her the dhamma. She was afterwards established in the fruition of the first stage of sanctification. Thereafter she entered the order under Mahapajapafi Gotami. She strove hard for insight and in course of time she won arhatship.

Tissa was born at Kapilavastu among the Sakyas. She renounced the world with Mahapajapati Gotami and became spiritually so developed that she attained arhatship. Sumedha, daughter of King Konca of Mantavati, was averse to the pleasures of senses from her childhood. She renounced the world hearing the doctrine of the Buddha from the bhikkhunis. Very soon she acquired insight and attained arhatship.

Visakha was the daughter of Sumanadevi, wife of Dhananjayasetthi, son of Mundakasetthi. Her abode was at Bhaddiyanagara in the kingdom of Anga. When seven years old Buddha with the bhikkhusamgha went to Bhaddiyanagara. Sumanadevi was one of the advisers of the king. Visakha with 500 female companions and 500 chariots received Buddha, who gave instructions to her according to her nature and she obtained sotapattiphalam. The Buddha was invited to Visakha's house. Visakha who was endowed with five kinds of beauty was married to Punnavaddhana of Savatthi.

The presents sent by the citizens of Savatthi for her, were distributed by her among the citizens with great courtesy. She made the citizens her own relatives. She refused to salute the naked heretics who were worshipped by her father-in-law. Her father-in-law was converted to Buddhism through her efforts. Once Visakha invited the bhikkhus and her father-in-law on hearing the sermon obtained sotapattiphalam.

On the death of her grandchild, who was very dear to her, Visakha went to see the Buddha with wet clothes and wet hair. The Buddha asked her whether she would be satisfied if all the people of Savatthi became her sons and grandsons. She replied in the affirmative. The Master asked her as to how many people met with their death at Savatthi. Visakha said from one to ten. The Buddha told her, " Just think whether you would be free from wet clothes and wet hair". Visakha said that she did not want so many sons and grandsons, because acquisition of more sons and grandsons would bring greater suffering.

Visakha, mother of Migara, was the foremost of the female supporters of the Buddha. Once on a sabbath day she went to the Buddha while the latter was in her palace named Pubbarama. Buddha instructed Visakha thus, "There were three kinds of uposatha and the ariya uposatha is the best of the uposathas. The Master then said that in order to observe ariya uposatha one should meditate on the Buddha, Dhamma and Samgha. Silas must be unbroken and fully observed. One should also meditate on the qualities of gods. One should follow Arhats who follow precepts throughout their lives. By observing ariya uposatha one may obtain great happiness and may be reborn in one of the heavens commencing from the Catumaharajika to the Paranimmittavasavatti and enjoy great celestial happiness there.

Visakha was further instructed by the Buddha thus, "Dependence on others is suffering, independence brings happiness". Visakha once blamed the bhikkhus for not allowing her grandson to be ordained during the lent, as owing to this delay her grandson's mind was changed. She once went to the Buddha and invited him together with the bhikkhus to take food at her house the next morning. Heavy rains fell on the following morning and the bhikkhus, as they had no bathing costumes, bathed themselves naked. Visakha came to know this fact from her maid servant who was sent to call the bhikkhus.

The Buddha together with the bhikkhus came to her house. She fed the Buddha, and the bhikkhus satisfactorily. After they had finished their meal, Visakha prayed to the Buddha for the following boons:--As long as she lived, she would give garments for the rainy season to the bhikkhus, food to the guests and food to those going abroad, diet to the sick bhikkhus, food to the sick-- nurses, medicine for the sick bhikkhus, rice gruel to the bhikkhus daily and bathing garments to the bhikkhunis. From this fact it is evident that Visakha introduced bathing garments for the bhikkhunis. It was Visakha who offered to the Buddha a napkin which he accepted.

We are further informed that Visakha, as soon as she heard of the advent of the quarrelsome Kosambian bhikkhus, approached the Buddha to take his advice as to how she should deal with them. The Buddha advised her to offer charities to the two parties of the quarrelsome Kosambian monks. Visakha prepared a golden water-pot for the Buddha. A samanera named Sumana brought water in that pot for the Buddha from Anotatta lake. She offered a water pot and a broom to the Buddha, which he accepted and also instructed the bhikkhus to use them. Once she went to the Buddha and offered a palm-leaf fan, which he accepted. Visakha was so very kind to the bhikkhus that she built a mansion for them, The bhikkhus at first hesitated to use it, but afterwards asked for Buddha's permission which was granted.

Visakha once went to the hermitage of Khadiravaniyarevata, but she found it to be in the midst of thorns and not fit for human habitation. Visakha was an important personage, because among the Bhikkhus if there were any matter for reference, it was referred to her, as we find in the case of Kundadhanathera who used to walk about with a woman behind him. In the family of Visakha young girls used to serve the Bhikkhus by making arrangements for their food, etc. Visakha's son's daughter named Datta who was entrusted with the care of the Bhikkhusamgha died in her absence. Visakha was very much afflicted with grief. The Buddha, consoled her.

Visakha was one day going to the city garden wearing all sorts of rich ornaments amongst which may be mentioned mahalata, an ornament of extraordinary beauty and of immense value. On the way she thought why should she go to the city garden like a mere girl; it was better that she should go to-the Vihara and listen to the discourses of the Buddha. Moved by the thought, she went to the Lord, put off her ornament, mahalata and gave it to her maid-servant to keep it and return it when she came out of the Vihara. Thereafter she listened to the noble discourses of the Buddha. On coming out of the Vihara, she asked for her ornament. The maid-servant said that she had left it in the Vihara. Both of them returned to the Vihara and found it. Visakha offered it to the Lord, and under his directions built a Vihara with the sale proceeds of the ornament, which amounted to nine crores and a lakh. Visakha offered to her maid-servant all the merit that accrued for constructing the Vihara. The latter approved of her charity and died shortly afterwards.

Anula was the queen of the king of Ceylon. Surrounded by five hundred girls, she bowed to the theras and honoured them to her heart's content. Thera Mahinda preached dhamma to them. Peta stories, Vimana stories and Saccasamyutta more narrated to them. When they heard the most excellent portion of the doctrine, princess Anula and her five hundred attendants attained sotapatti. She became a believer in the Buddha, Dhamma and the Samgha. With her five hundred attendants she received the Pabbajja ordination from Samghamitta Mahatheri.

Gopika was a Sakya princess. She was pleased with the Buddha, Dhamma and Samgha. She used to observe precepts fully, became disgusted with female life and meditated in order to become a man.

Canda came of a Brahman family. She earned her living by begging from door to door. One day she came to the spot where Patacara had just finished her meal. The bhikkhunis saw her hungry and gave her some food to eat. She ate the food and took her seat on one side. She then listened to the discourse of the Theri and renounced the world. She practised hard to attain-insight. Her knowledge matured and her determination was strong. Hence she succeeded in attaining arhatship with patisambhida.

Gutta came of a Brahman family at Savatthi. In her youth household life became repugnant to her. She obtained her parents' consent and entered the order under Mahapajapati Gotami. Thereafter she could not for sometime control her mind from external interests. Then the Master gave her suitable instructions, and she attained arhatship together with patisambhida.

Vijaya came of a certain clansmen's family of Rajagaha. She was a friend of Khema. When she heard that Khema, a king's consort, had renounced the world, she went to Khema, who taught her the Norm and ordained her. Very soon she won insight and after a short time attained arhatship with analytical knowledge. Mara came, to tempt her by saying, "You are young and beautiful, I am also young and beautiful, let us enjoy ourselves with music." She replied, "I find delight in rupa, sadda, gandha, etc. and I don't like soft-touch. I hate very much my rotten body which is easily destructible. My ignorance is dispelled." Then Mara left her.

Cala, Upacala and Sisupacala were born in Magadha at the village of Nalaka as the children of a Brahmani named Surupasari. They were younger sisters of Sariputta. When they heard that their brother had left the world for the order, they too renounced the world and striving hard, attained arhatship. In vain Mara tried to stir up sensual desires in them.

Uppalavanna came of a banker's family at Savatthi. Her skin was of the colour of the heart (gabbha) of the blue lotus. Hence she was called Uppalavanna. Many princes and banker's sons wanted to marry her. But she renounced the world, went to the bhikkhunis and was ordained. Thereafter one day she lighted a lamp, and by continually contemplating on the flame of the lamp, she gradually obtained arhatship with adhinna and patisambhida. She was assigned a chief place among those who had the gift of iddhi.

The Samyutta Nikaya tells us that Theri Uppalavanna went to Andhavana to meditate. There she sat at the foot of the Sala tree. Mara came to her and said to her, "You are Sitting at the foot of a fully blossomed Sala tree, are you not afraid of the wicked?" She replied, "I do not care for the wicked. I do not care for you." Mara left her. After defeating Mara, Uppalavanna was molested by her maternal uncle's son Ananda, who was enamoured of her beauty and who wanted to marry her. Although Uppalavanna had become a bhikkhuni, Ananda could not give up the desire of marrying her. Once Ananda concealed himself in the room of the Theri under her bedstead in her absence.

When the Theri returned home and lay herself down on the bedstead, Ananda suddenly came out and committed rape on her. The Theri informed the bhikkhunis of this fact, and through the bhikkhunis brought this to the notice of the Buddha, who prohibited the bhikkhunis from living in forests. Uppalavanna Theri acquired the power of performing a miracle by coming in to the presence of the Buddha to worship him with the pomp and grandeur of an individual monarch, being surrounded by a retinue extending over 36,000 yojanas and this miracle was visible to an assembly extending over twelve yojanas.

Sumangalamata came of a poor family of Savatthi. She was married to a basket maker. She acquired great merit. One day while reflecting on all she had suffered, she was much affected and her insight quickening, she attained arhatship with analytical knowledge. Punna or Punnika acquired great merit in her previous birth, but owing to her pride she could not root out klesas (sins). She was born of a domestic slave at Savatthi in the household of Anathapindika, the banker. She obtained sotapattiphalam after hearing the Sihanada Suttanta. Afterwards Anathapindika gave her freedom because she defeated a Brahman named Udakasuddhika. Punna renounced worldly life and entered the order. She practised insight and very soon attained arhatship with patisambhida.

Sundari was born at Benares as the daughter of Sujata, a Brahman. On her brother's death, her father became overwhelmed with grief. With the advice of Theri Vasitthi her father renounced the world, met the Buddha at Mithila, entered the order and in course of time attained arhatship. Sundari heard of her father's renouncing the world. She sacrificed all her wealth and pleasures of all kinds. She secured her mother's consent to leave the world. She then entered the order and striving hard she attained arhatship with patisambhida.

Vimala was born at Vesali as the daughter of a public woman. When advanced in years she was moved to see one day the venerable Mahamoggallana going about for alms. She went to his house to entice him. Mahamoggallana rebuked her. She was ashamed and became a believer and lay sister. Sometime affer she entered the order and very soon attained arhatship.

Mittakalika came of a Brahman's family in the town of Kammasadamma in the kingdom of the Kurus. When she grew up she one day heard the teaching of the Great Discourse on the Mahasatipatthana and entered the order of sisters. For seven years she could not elevate herself intellectually. Later on she won arhatship together with analytical knowledge.

Sakula (Pakula) was born in a Brahman family at Savatthi. Seeing the Master accepting the gift of the Jetavana, she became a believer. One day she heard the preaching of an arhat and was greatly convinced. She entered the order, strove hard for insight and soon won arhatship. She was given the foremost place by the Master among the bhikkhunis possessing divine eyes.

Sonadinna, a female devotee living in Nalanda used to serve the bhikkhus with the four requisites and used to observe the precept and uposatha with perfect regularity. She meditated on the four noble truths and attained sotapatti. Aloma, a poor woman living at Savatthi in Benares not finding anything to offer, presented some rotten cooked rice without salt to the Buddha who accepted it.

Mutta came of a rich Brahman family of Savatthi. When she was twenty years old, she went to Mahapajapati the Gotami and got ordination from her. She was practising kammatthana and she was instructed by the Buddha to get herself free from all bonds. Afterwards she became an arhat.

Punna was the daughter of a leading burgess of Savatthi, When she was about twenty years of age, she heard the great Pajapati teach the doctrine, and renounced the world. She practised insight, being encouraged by the Master. In due course she attained arhatship.

Dantika came of a purohita's family at Kosala. When she came of age, she acquired faith in the Buddha in the Jetavana, and later entered the order under Mahapajapati Gotami at Rajagaha. While staying at Rajagaha, she climbed the Vulture's Peak after her meal, and while resting she developed insight and soon obtained arhatship with analytical knowledge.

Vaddhesi was the nurse of Mahapajapati Gotami. When her mistress renounced the world, she followed her. For twenty-five years she was harassed by the lusts of the senses and failed to acquire concentration of mind. One day she heard Dhammadinna preach the Norm. She then began to practise meditation. Very soon she acquired the six supernatural powers.

Uttama came of a householder family at Bandhumati. When she grew old, she heard Patacara preach and entered the order. When Patacara gave her admonition, she was established in insight and very soon won arhatship.

Thirty sisters born in different families of different places heard Patacara preach and were converted by her and entered the order. They practised insight and in course of time they won arhatship with patisambhida.

Uttara came of a certain clansmen's family at Savatthi. When grown up she heard Patacara preach the Norm. She became a believer, entered the Order and became an arhat.

Uttari was a theri who was 120 years old. She went to beg for alms. Once, while going for alms, she met the Buddha on the way and when going to salute him, she fell down. The Buddha delivered a sermon to her, and she having attained the first stage of sanctification died.

Khujjuttara was the maid servant of Samavati, queen of King Udena of Kosambi. Her daily duty was to buy flowers from Sumana, a garland-maker for eight kahapanas. Once the Buddha together with the bhikkhusamgha was invited to take meals in Sumana's house. Khujjuttara waited on her and heard the sermon delivered by the Buddha. She obtained sotapattiphalam after hearing the sermon. In former days she used to steal four kahapanas out of eight kahapanas given to her by her mistress for buying flowers. After having obtained sotapattiphalam she brought flowers to the value of eight kahapanas. She confessed her guilt when asked why she brought such a large quantity of flowers. She told Samavati that she had acquired knowledge and came to realise that stealing things is a sin committed by a person who listened to the Buddha's sermon. Samavati after listening to the dhamma repeated by her obtained sotapattiphalam. She was well versed in Tripitaka.

Dinna was an upaisika of the Buddha. She was the queen of King Uggasena. A king promised to the deity of a nigrodha tree that he would worship the deity with the blood of one hundred kings of Jambudipa if he got the throne after his father's death. He then defeated all the kings gradually and went to worship the deity, but the deity, seeing that many kings would be killed, being compassionate to them, refused his worship on the ground that the queen of King Uggasena whom he had defeated was not brought. The king had her brought, and she preached a sermon on the avoidance of life--slaughter in their presence. The deity approved and the king refrained from life-slaughter, and released the defeated and captured kings, who praised Dinna for this act. It was due to her that so many kings were saved.

Sona came of a clansmen's family at Savatthi. In course of time, after marriage, she became the mother of ten sons and was known as Bahuputtika. The Dhammapada Commy. says that she had seven sons and seven daughters.

On her husband renouncing the world she divided all her riches equally between her sons. In a very short time her sons and daughters-in-law ceased to show respect. She then entered the Order of the bhikkhunis and began to practise insight strenuously in her old age. The master gave her suitable instructions. Sona Bhikkhuni then attained arhatship.

She occupied the foremost place among the bhikkhunis, making great exertion.

Bhadda Kundalakesa came of the family of a banker at Rajagaha. When grown up, she one day saw Satthuka, the purohita's son, being led to execution by the city guard. She fell in love with him at first sight. She resolved to die if she did not get him. Her father heard of this and got Satthuka released by bribing the guard heavily. Satthuka was brought to Bhadda, who, decked in jewels, waited upon him. He saw her jewels and coveted them. He told Bhadda to get ready an offering to be given to the cliff deity. Bhadda did so. She adorned herself with all her jewels and accompanied her husband to the precipice with an offering. On reaching the top of the precipice, Satthuka told her to put off all her ornaments which he had come there to take. In vain Bhadda pleaded that She herself and all her ornaments belonged to him. Satthuka did not take any notice of her pleadings. He wanted all her ornaments. Bhadda then prayed for an embrace with all her jewels on.

Satthuka granted her prayer. Bhadda embraced him in front and then, as if embracing him from the back, pushed him over the precipice. Satthuka died. Thereafter Bhadda did not come home, but she left the world and entered the Order of the Niganthas. She learnt the doctrine of the Niganthas and left their company. Thereafter she found no one equal to her in debate. She setup the branch of a jambu tree on a heap of sand at the gate of some village or town, with the declaration that any body able to join issue with her in debate should trample on this bough. Sariputta ordered some children who were near the bough, to trample on it. The children did so. When Bhadda saw the bough trampled, she challenged Sariputa to a debate before some Sakyan recluses and was advised to go to Buddha for refuge. She went to the Buddha who discerned the maturity of her knowledge. Buddha spoke a verse and she attained arhatship with analytical knowledge. Bhadda was assigned a chief place among the bhikkhunis possessing ready wit.

Sama came of a rich householder's family at Kosambi. She was moved by the death of her dear friend, the lay-disciple Samavati. One day she listened to Elder Ananda preaching and acquired insight. On the seventh day after this she attained arhatship with a thorough grasp of the Dhamma in form and meaning.

Another Sama who came of a clansmen's family at Kosambi, was a friend of Samavati, whose death afflicted her so much that she could not gain self-control for twenty-five years. In her old age she heard a sermon through which her insight expanded and she won arhatship with patisambhida (analytical knowledge).

Ubbiri came of the family of a rich house- holder at Savatthi. She was very beautiful, and was brought to the palace by the king of Kosala. A few years later a daughter was born to her. This daughter was named Jiva. The king saw the child and was very much pleased. He then had Ubbiri anointed as queen. After a few years Jiva died. The mother used to go to the cemetery and shed tears. Questioned by the Exalted One as to why she was weeping, she said that she was shedding tears for her deceased daughter. She was questioned by the Exalted One as to which of the 84,000. daughters she was weeping for. She then spent a little thought and intelligence over the Norm thus taught by the Buddha. She was established in insight, and in due course she won arhatship by virtue of great merits.

Kisagotami came of poor family at Savatthi. She was married to a rich banker's son who had forty crores of wealth. Bodhisatta was her maternal uncle's son. One day, while the Bodhisatta was returning home after receiving the news of Rahula's birth, he was seen by Kisagotami from her palace. Buddha's beauty pleased Kisagotami so much that she uttered a stanza, the purport of which is, "the mother who has such a child and the father who has such a son and the wife who has such a husband are surely happy" (nibbuta), but the Bodhisatta took the word nibbuta in the sense of nibbanam. The Bodhisatta presented her with a pearl necklace for making him hear such auspicious and sacred words.

On the death of her only child she went to the Buddha with the dead body and requested him to bring the dead to life. Buddha asked her to bring a little mustard seed from a house where no man had died. Kisagotami went from house to house, but she came back to Buddha quite unsuccessful. The Buddha delivered a sermon which led her to become a bhikkhuni. Her insight grew within a short time and she attained arhatship. Then the master assigned her the foremost place among the bhikkhunis who used very rough and simple robes. Once Kisagotami went to Andhavana to meditate. Mara, came to her and said," You have killed your sons and now you are crying. Why are you not searching for another man? " Kisagotami replied, "I have completely destroyecl my sons and my husband and I have no sorrow. I am not afraid of you, my attachment is destroyed and ignorance is dispelled. Killing the army of death I live sinless." Mara then left her.

Once Kisagotami was coming through the sky to worship the Buddha while Sakka with his retinue was seated before the Buddha. She did not come to the Buddha, but worshipped him from the sky and went away. Being questioned by Sakka, the Buddha answered that she was his daughter.Kisagotami, who was the foremost among the bhikkhunis, used very rough and simple robes.

Patacara came of a banker's family at Savatthi. In her youth she formed an intimacy with a servant of her house. On the day fixed for her marriage with another youth of equal rank she eloped with her lover and dwelt in a hamlet. There she used to perform household duties, and her lover used to bring wood from the forest and work in a field belonging to others. Shortly afterwards Patacara gave birth to a child, but at the time of the birth of her second child, a storm arose. Her husband went to a forest to cut grass and sticks. While he cut a stake standing on an ant-hill, a snake came from the ant-hill and bit him. He fell there and died. The next morning Patacara went to the forest with her two children and found her husband dead. She lamented and left the place.

On her way to her father's house there was a river, the water of which was knee-deep. She lost her children while crossing the river. With tears of grief she came to Savatthi and learnt that her parents and brother had perished under the debris of the fallen house. She turned mad. Since then she did not wear clothing, and was therefore known as Patacara. One day the Exalted One saw her in that plight and said, "Sister! Cover your shamelessness." She regained her consciousness, and the Lord taught her that sons, parents and kinsfolk were no shelter, and asked her to discern this truth in order to make clear quickly the way to nibbana. Then she was established in the sotapattiphalam. She attained arhatship with analytical knowledge.

Thereafter she preached the Buddha's dhamma and converted many afflicted women to the Buddhist faith. The Therigatha Commy. says that Patacara had five hundred female disciples, who came of different families of different places. They were married, bore children and lived domestic lives. Overwhelmed with grief at the loss of children they went to Patacara, who asked them not to weep when the manner of birth and death was unkown to them. They were greatly moved by Patacara's teachings and renounced the world under her. They performed exercises for insight and soon became established in arhatship with patisambhida.

Vasitthi came of a clansmen's family at Vaisali. Her parents gave her in marriage to a clansman's son of equal position. She had a son. When the child was able to run about, he died. Vasitthi went mad with grief. She came to Mithila and there she saw the Exalted One, self-controlled and self-contained. At the sight of the Buddha the frenzy left her and she recovered her normal mind. The master taught her the outlines of the Norm. Performing all proper duties, she acquired insight, and struggling with the help of full Knowledge, she soon attained arhatship together with a thorough grasp of the Norm in form and spirit.

Dhammadinna came of a clansmen's family at Rajagaha and became the wife of a Setthi named Visakha. One day her husband heard the master teaching, and after hearing him he did not hold converse with her as he used to do before, but renounced the worldly life. Dhammadinna too became a bhikkhuni and took up her residence in a village. One of the great merits acquired in her previous births was her subjugation of the complexities of thought, word and deed. By virtue of this merit, she soon attained arhatship together with thorough mastery of the form and meaning of the Dhamma. Then she returned to Rajagaha and was questioned by her husband on the khandas and the like. She answered so correctly that she was praised by the Buddha and was ranked as foremost among the sisters who could preach.

Dhamma came of a respectable family at Savatthi. Given in marriage to a suitable husband, she became converted. On her husband's death, she entered the Order. In due course she won arhatship with thorough knowledge of the Norm in form and meaning. Mettika was the daughter of a rich Brahman of Rajagaha. She climbed a hill and lived like a recluse. She acquired insight and within a short time won arhatship.

She was a friend of Abhayamata. She followed her in renouncing the world, and entered the Order. In course of time she attained arhatship at Rajagaha.

Soma was born at Rajagaha as the daughter of the purohita of King Bimbisara. When advanced in years she became a lay disciple. Afterwards she entered the order of the bhikkhunis. She performed exercises of insight and within a short time won arhatship. Mara tried in vain to divert her from this path. From the Samyutta Nikaya we learn that Mara came to her and said,"What is to be obtained by the Rishis, you are, with slight wisdom, trying to have it. That which is difficult to be obtained by great sages, you being a silly woman, want to have." She replied: " If my mind is steadfast, I must acquire it, my womanly nature will not prevent me from acquiring it." Mara then left her.

Bhadda Kapilani came of a Brahman family of the Kosiya clan at Sagala. She was married to a young noble Pippali at the village of Mahatittha. When her husband renounced the world, she made over her wealth to her kinsfolk. She then left the world and dwelt five years in the hermitage of the heretics. Thereafter, she was ordained by Mahapajapati Gotami. Establishing insight she soon won arhatship. By the master she was ranked first among the bhikkhunis who could remember previous births. Besides the women who embraced a homeless life and became bhikkhunis and theris, there were others who were staunch believers in the Buddha's dhamma. These women used to lead a domestic life, offering charities in the shape of coin and kind to theras, bhikkhunis and bhikkhus in the expectation of a happier rebirth or for the benefit of departed relations. The incidents in the life of some of these women are recorded in the Buddhist literature, and it would not be out of place here to mention them below. Uttara, daughter of Nandaka, Commander-in-chief

of Pingala, king of Surattha, was a believer in the Buddha. She used to offer to a saintly thera cold and perfumed drink as well as excellent cake and sweets for the benefit of her departed father.

Lakhuma lived near one of the gates of Benares. She used to offer a spoonful of rice to the bhikkhus when they entered the town by that gate. Thus she acquired the habit of offering charity. In the asanasala (rest house), she used to prepare seats for, and supply water to, the bhikkhus. She was established in sotapatti. After death she was reborn in the Tavatimsa heaven.

A daughter of a certain upasaka of Rajagaha was very much devoted to Mahamoggallana. One day she welcomed a thera, offered him a seat, worshipped him with a garland of sumana flower and gave him sweets, etc. On her death, she was reborn in the Tavatimsa heaven.

Mallilka was the daughter of a Brahman steward of the Sakya Mahanaman. On her father's death she was taken by Mahanaman to his house. She was at first named Chandra. She made a wreath which satisfied Mahanaman so much that he changed her name to Mallika. One day Mallika went to the garden with her food, and just then the Blessed One passed them collecting alms. Mallika thought of offering her food to the Buddha, and the latter knowing her thought held out his bowl. She put her offering in it and wished at the same time that some day she might be free from slavery or poverty. One day Pasenadi carried away by his horse in the heat of the chase came to Mahanaman's garden. There he saw Mallika. Re- quested by the king, Mallika rubbed his feet with a towel. As soon as she did so the king fell asleep. When he awoke he found out who she was, went to Mahanaman and married her. She was then taken to Sravasti and in time she brought forth a son named Virudhaka, and also a daughter. This story is nothing but a Tibetan version of the story of Pase- nādi and Vasabhakhattiya.

Again we read that Mallikadevi went to the Buddha and asked him thus, "What is the cause of a woman's getting an ugly appearance, bad habit, wretched state and poverty in this world? What is the cause of a woman who is of this nature becoming very rich and influential? What is the cause of a woman who is of good appearance and lovely becoming poor and uninfluential, and vice versa? "The Buddha answered thus: " The woman who is very hot-tempered and who gets angry for slight reason becomes poor and ugly if she does not offer any charity to the Samanas or Brahmanas, but if she offers charity to the Samanas or Brahamanas, she becomes rich and influential alth- ough she is hot-tempered."

The Buddha further said "She who is not hot-tempered and does not become angry for slight reason becomes poor and influential if she does not offer any charity to the Samanas or Brahmanas." Mallika admitted that on account of her hot-temper and peevish nature she had an ugly appearance, but she, on account of her previous charities, became a queen. She further said that she would treat properly the daughter of the Ksatriyas, the Brahmanas and the other householders who were subordinate to her. She became a devotee of the Buddha, being very pleased with him.

It is noteworthy that once Mallika was asked by Pasenadi whether she had anybody dearer to her than her own soul. She replied in the negative. Pasenadi was asked the same question by his wife, and he too answered it in the negative. She then went to the Buddha and related the matter to him. The Buddha said that they were right in holding that there was nothing more favourite than one's own soul.

Once Pasenadi invited Buddha to teach Dhamma to queens Mallika and Vasabhakhattiya as they were desirous of learning it. Buddha asked the king to engage Ananda for the purpose as it was not possible for him to go every day. Mallikadevi learnt it thoroughly, but Vasabhakhattiya was not so mindful of learning Dhamma. It was Mallika who saved the life of many living beings who were brought for sacrifice to save Pasenadi from the evil effect of hearing four horrible sounds at midnight by inducing him to go to the Buddha to take instructions from him. After her death, Mallikadevi had to suffer in the Avici hell because she deceived her husband by telling a lie about her misconduct.

Mallikadevi made the following arrangements on the occasion of Pasenadi's offering a unique gift to the Buddha and the bhikkhus:

1. She made a canopy with Sala wooden parts, under which five hundred bhikkhus could sit within the parts and five hundred outside them.
2. Five hundred white umbrellas were raised by five hundred elephants standing at the back of five hundred bhikkhus.
3. Golden boats were placed in the middle of the pandal, and each Khattiya, daughter threw scents standing in the midst of the two bhikkhus.
4. Each Khattiya princess fanned standing in the midst of two bhikkhus.
5. Golden boats were filled with scents and perfumes.

The daughter of queen Mallika was also named Mallika. She was the wife of General Bandhula. She was childless for a long time. Bandhula sent her to her father's house. On the way she went to the Jetavana to salute the Buddha who was informed by her that her husband was sending her home as she was childless. The Buddha asked her to go to her husband's house. Bandhula was informed of this fact and thought that the Buddha must have got the idea that she would be pregnant. The sign of pregnancy was visible in her, and she desired to drink water and bathe in the well-guarded tank of the Licchavis. Bandhula with his wife visited the tank and he made his wife bathe and drink water therefrom. Mallika, wife of Bandhula, and daughter of a Malla king of Kusinara, offered worship to the relic of the Buddha with plenty of perfumes and garlands and also an ornament named mahalata which was very valuable. In consequence of this, she, after death, was reborn in the Tavatimsa heaven where she was bedecked all in yellow.

Vajira was a bhikkuni who was tempted by Mara when she went to Andhavana to meditate. Mara came to her and asked her, " Who has created the being? Wherefrom it has come, and. where will it go?" She said, "The aggregation of five khandhas constitutes the sattas." Mara then left her.

Cira bhikkhuni was given a robe by an upasika of the Buddha. This message was declared by a Yakkha in the streets of Rajagaha saying that the giver by giving a robe to Cira who was free from fetters, could acquire much merit.

Uttara and her husband were serving a banker at Rajagaha. Once the banker went to attend a famous ceremony, and Uttttra with her husband was at home. The husband of Uttara went to cultivate in the morning. Uttara was going with cooked food to her husband in the field. On the way she met Sariputta who was just rising up from nirodha-samapatti (meditation on cessrttion) and offered the food to him, with the result that she became the richest lady of Rajagaha, and her husband became a banker named Mahadhanasetthi.

Punna was the maid-servant of a banber of Savatthi. Once she was asked to husk a large quantity of paddy. While engaged in husking the paddy at night, she went outside the house to take rest. At this time Dabba, a Mallian, was in charge of making arrangements for the sleeping accommodation of the bhikkhus who were guests. Punna with some cakes went out to enquire of the cause of their movements with lights at night. The Buddha went out for alms by the way in which Punna was. She offered all the cakes to the Buddha without keeping any for herself. The Buddha accepted them. Punna was thinking whether Buddha would partake of her food. The Buddha did partake of it in her house. The effect of this offer was that Punna obtained sotapattiphalam where the offer was made.

Rohini was Anuruddha's sister. She was suffering from white leprosy. She did not go to her brother as she was suffering. Anuruddha sent for her and asked her to build a rest- house for bhikkhus to get rid of her sin. She kept the rest-house clean even when if was under construction, and she did this with great devotion for a long time. She became free from her disease. Shortly afterwards the Buddha went to Kapilavatthu and sent for Rohini. The Buddha told her that she was the queen of the king of Benares in her former birth. The king was enamoured of the beauty of a dancing girl. The queen knowing this, became jealous of her, and to punish her she put something in her cloth and bathing water which produced terrible itching all over her body. On account of this sin, she got this disease. She obtained sotapattiphalam and the colour of her body became golden.

Suppavasa, a daughter of a Koliyan was pregnant for seven years, but she did not give birth to any child. After seven years, labour pain began and she sufffered terribly for seven days, but no child was born. She requested her husband to go to the Buddha and to salute him on her behalf, reporting the matter to him. Her husband went to the Buddha and informed him. The Buddha desired that Suppavasa would give birth to a son without any pain and disease. While the Buddha was expressing this desire, a son was born. Her husband was sent again to invite the Buddha to her house for seven days. The Buddha accepted the invitation. The Master took his meal there for seven days and converted both of them. Suppavasa used to give alms daily to five hundred bhikkhus. She became the foremost of the upasikas, offering the best food to the Buddha. Buddha told her the good effect of offering food, and he further said that an offerer by offering rice offers the lease of life, beauty , happiness and strength. The offerer in return obtains celestial life, celestial beauty, happiness and strength.

Another bhikkhuni of some repute was Nakulamata. When her husband was ill and was ready to die, free from anxiety, she told him that she knew spinning and weaving and management of household affairs and children. She also told her husband that she would never remarry after his death, as both of them lived the life of a recluse for sixteen years. She informed her husband that after his death she would meet the Buddha and the bhikkhusamgha. She also promised to observe the precepts. She also told her husband that she was one of the female devotees who fully observed the precepts, controlled the mind, had strong faith in the Buddha, Dhamma and Samgha, and who became fearless and did not depend on others except the Buddha for support.

Bojjha was a devotee who approached the Buddha, who preached to her the reward of observing the precepts and the Sabbath. The Master said to her. "Happiness obtained by observing Sabbath is sixteen times greater than that enjoyed by the sixteen countries."

Velukantaki Nandamata was a devotee of the Buddha. She gave offerings to Sariputta and Moggallana. Referring to this the Buddha said, "A giver must be pleased before he gives dana; his mind must be pleased while giving dana and after giving dana. The receiver of the offering must be free from passion, hatred and delusion. The consequence of such a gift is immeasurable". Nandamata gave such a gift to Sariputta and Moggallana, and she obtained immeasurable consequence of the gift. There was another bhikkhuni named Nandamata who was once repeating the Parayana Sutta of the Sutta Nipata in a sweet voice. King Vessavana was going from north to south, and he waited there till Nandamata finished her repetition and praised her much.

Nandamata told Vessavans that the merit acquired by the act would he beneficial to him. Vessavana gladly assented and said that the merit which would be acquired by her through the gift made to Sariputta and Moggallana would prove beneficial to him.

Migasala was an upasika who went to Ananda and said, "According to the instruction of the Buddha, a brahmacari and an abrahamacari go to the same place after death and enjoy the same amount of happiness." Ananda went to the Buddha to have this problem solved. The Buddha said that the lay devotee was ignorant and uneducated and therefore she could not realize it properly. The Buddha further said, "Even a householder may acquire the same amount of merit as acquired by a brahmacari who does not fulfil his duties properly."

Dinna, a bhikkhuni, was asked by her husband about sakkayaditthi, sakkayanirodha, ariyatthangikamaggo, samkhara, nirodhasamapatti, manner of rising up from nirodhasamapatti and vedana. Dhammadina gave satisfactory answers to all the questions. She said, "Five upadana khandhas constitute, sakkayaditthi. Tanha means sakkaya samudayo. Destruction of tanha means sakkaya nirodha. The noble eight-fold path is the means of attaining sakkayanirodha. Ignorant people take the five upadana khandhas jointly and separately as atta (soul); the learned and noble disciples do not take them in this sense. Those who obtain nirodha samapatti are stopped one after another. The three kinds of vedana are sukha, dukkha and adukkhamasukha.

There was an Upasika named Suyata who destroyed three bonds and obtained the first stage of sanctification. Nanda, sister of the king of Kosala, was a bhikkhuni. While going through the sky at night she instructed Kalasoka and bhikkhusamgha to purify bhikkhusamgha by driving out had bhikkhus and protecting good bhikkhus.

There was another woman named Nanda who was the wife of a householder named Nandasena who lived in a certain village near Savatthi. She had no faith in the Buddha. Sho was very hot-tempered and used to abuse her husband, father-in-law and mother-in-law. On her death she became a peti. One day she appeared before her husband and gave him an account of her past misdeeds. The husband made gifts for her sake to the bhikkhus, and Nanda was released from her miseries.

Revati was the daughter of a householder of Benares. She had no faith in the Buddha, and was very uncharitable. For some days she was forced by her parents to do meritorious deeds in order to win Nandiya, a neighbour's son, as her husband. After marriage, Nandiya made her follow him in his meritorious deeds. Thereafter Nandiya had to go abroad. He asked his wife to continue all the meritorious deeds. Revati did so for seven days. Then she stopped all meritorious deeds and began to abuse the bhikkhus who had come to her house for alms. Nandiya, on his return, found that all his acts of charity had been discontinued. After death Revati became a hellish creature. On his death Nandiya became a devata. He saw with his divine eyes that Revati had become a hellish creature. He then went to her and asked her to approve of the meritorious acts done by him. As soon as she did so, she became a devata and resided with Nandiya in heaven.

Samavati was the queen of king Udena of Kosambi. The harem containing Samavati with 500 female attendants was burnt while Udena was in the royal garden. The matter was referred to the Buddha, who said, " Each upasika had gone according to her kamma, some have become sotapanna sakadagami and anagami and so forth.

There was a maid-servant named Birani engaged by Asoka Brahmana to give food daily to the samgha which was enough for eight bhikkhus. This she used to do with devotion, with the result that after her death she was born in avimana in the sky.

Rupananda was Buddha's step-sister. She thought that her eldest brother renounced the world and had become a Buddha. Her younger brother Nanda was a bhikkhu and Rahulakumara had obtained ordination. Her husband too became a bhikkhu and her mother, Mahapajapatigotami, became a bhikkhuni. She renounced the world thinking that sc many of her relatives had renounced the world. she did not go before the Buddha as she was proud of her beauty, while the Buddha used to preach the impermanency and worthlessness of form. The other bhikkhunis and bhikkhus always used to praise the Buddha in her presence and tell her that all having different tastes became blessed by seeing the Buddha.

Nanda thought of going to the Buddha with other bhikkhunis but she would not show herself to the Buddha. Ananda came to know that Nanda had come with the bhikkhunis. The Buddha desired to lower her pride in her beauty by showing the bad effect of it. By his miraculous power the Buddha created a most beautiful girl who was engaged in fanning the Buddha. Nanda seeing her beauty found out that her own beauty was much inferior. The girl was seen gradually attaining youth, the state of a mother of a child and then old age and disease and death. Nanda, seeing this, gave up her pride in her beauty and came to realize the impermanence of beauty. The Buddha, knowing the state of her mind, delivered a suitable sermon and she became an arhat after hearing it.

CHINESE BHIKSUNIS IN THE CH'AN TRADITION

The spirit of essential Mahayana Buddhist doctrines assumes equality between male and female, although in the mundane world the position of Buddhist women is lower than that of Buddhist men. The Chinese Ch'an Buddhist tradition, following the egalitarian teaching of One-Mind of enlightenment, advocates non-discriminating, universal Buddhahood accessible to every sentient being, whether male or female.

Nevertheless, women's status and spiritual capacities have not been upheld as highly in Buddhist history as they have by the Chinese Ch'an School. Although the Buddha acknowledges that "women, having gone forth from home into homelessness in the Dharma and discipline proclamined by the Truth-finder, are able to realize the fruit of stream-attainment or the fruit of once-returning or the fruit of non-returning or perfection,"1 women have not been regarded as equal in spiritual development in Buddhist literature.

Buddhist women in early Buddhism enjoyed a higher position than their later counterparts, yet in numerous early Buddhist texts they are portrayed as jealous, stupid, passionate and full of hatred. The prototypes for the negative image of women are the daughters of `Mara` , personified as Lust, Greed and Craving. Male practitioners who set their bodies and minds on the path to liberation were advised to keep women at a distance.2 Women are said to have five obstacles, namely being incapable of becoming a Brahma King, `Sakra` , King `Mara` , Cakravartin or Buddha. The body of woman is considered impure and shameful. In Mahayana literature we see a gradual evolution of a positive concept of women in terms of their wisdom and practice.

This change is based on the doctrine and philosophy of Mahayana Buddhism. Whereas the pre-Mahayana literature represents the traditional views of an established monastic institution dominated by monks, Mahayana adovcates the Bodhisattva figure who embodies the highest state of wisdom and compassion in which all sexual and social discrimination ceases to exist. Every one, whether male or female, monk or layperson, is regarded as a potential Buddha. However, the Mahayana literature, although propounding an egalitarian view, does not unanimously uphold the equal status of women. The spiritual status of women is presented differently from sutra to sutra within the Mahayana tradition. Generally speaking, the Mahayana sutras which depict women's spiritual progress may be classified into four types, illustrating the gradual improvement in the attitudes toward women.

The Sutras Which Hold a Negative Attitude toward Women

In these sutras women are protrayed as representing the profane world, `samsara`, and thus as potential obstacles to spiritual growth. In the `Udayanavatsaraja-parivartah` (The Tale of King Udayana of Vastasa) from the `Maharatnakuta` we read,

Women can destroy pure precepts.

They retreat from doing merits and honor.

Preventing others from rebirth in heaven,

They are the source of hell.5

The Ta-cheng Chou-hsiang kung-te ching (`Mahayana Stura` on the Merits of Making the Images of the Buddha) depicts women as narror-minded, jealous and hateful. They do not forgive nor repay kindness. Even if they seek enlightenment, they are not persistent. It is true that Mahayana was more sympathetic toward women, still the element of misogyny remained in some of its literature. However, this extreme prejudice against women is no longer the predominent attitude.

The Sutras which Deny a Women's Presence in the Buddhaland

The Pure Land scriptures are the most notable in this class. For example, the thirty-fourth vow of the `Larger Sukhavativyuha-sutra` states,

O Bhagavat, if, after I have obtained Bodhi, women in immeasurable, innumerable, inconceivable, immense Buddha countries on all sides after having heard my name, should allow carelessness to arise, should not turn their thoughts toward Bodhi, should, when they are free from birth, not despise their female nature, and if they being born again, should assume a second female nature, then may I not obtain the highest perfect knowledge."

The `Smaller Sukhavativyuha` also explicitly declares that there are no women in the Pure Land. Although the possibility of being born in the Pure Land is not denied to women, the implication here is that a male-nature is necessary for progress on the Bodhisattva path in the Pure Land.

The Sutras that Accept Women as Lower State Bodhisattvas

Most of the Mahayana sutras fall into this category. This includes such texts as the `Saddharmapundarika` , the `Sumatidarikapariprccha` , the `Astasaharikaprajna-paramita` , etc. In these sutras women are acknowledged as "good-knowing advisors" or spiritual "good friends" (`kalyanamitra`), but they are relegated to the lower Bodhisattva stages. To be consistent with the Mahayanist egalitarian view toward all sentient beings, the motif of sex transformation was introduced into these sutras. If a woman's virtue, merit and wisdom are extraordinary, she may, through a sex change, become a Bodhisattva or a Buddha in her present- or future life. Transformation of gender symbolizes a transition from the imperfect condition of a human being represented by the female body to the mental perfection of a Bodhisattva and Buddha represented by the male body. Thus, in response to the challenge from `Sariputra` , who represented the traditionally negative attitude toward women, the Dragon Girl in the `Lotus sutra` , who is depicted as very intelligent and having penetrated into the most profound Dharma, changes herself into a male Bodhisattva and then immediately becomes a Buddha.

Here the transformation of gender from female to male is a prerequisite for the Dragon Girl's realization of Buddhahood. Though the case of the Dragon Girl demonstrates the possibility of women's realization of Buddhahood, the notion of the dichotomy, namely, the notion of maleness and femaleness still exists.

The Sutras that accept Women as Advanced Bodhisattva and imminent Buddhas

The `Vimalakirti Sutra` and the `Srimala Sutra` belong to this category. In these two `sutras` the position of the female reaches its hightest peak. The doctrinal basis for this culmination lies in the Mahayana doctrines of `sunyata` (emptiness), `Tathagatagarbha` , non-duality, etc. Instead of attempting to identify maleness with Bodhisattvahood and Buddhahood, the sutras in this category claim that notions of duality--either male or female, subject or object, etc.--are merely mental attachments contradicting the teaching of emptiness.

The characteristics of "maleness" and "femaleness" are simply illusory and irrelevant. On this basis, the female bodhisattva refuses to undergo sexual change. When asked by `Sariputra` to transform herself, the Goddess in the

`Vimalakirti Sutra` said, "I have been here for twelve years and have looked for the innate characteristics of femaleness but have not been able to find them.-How can I change them?"8 Then the Goddess changed `Sariputra` into a female. This is to reinforce her assertion that every one and every thing transcends gender distinctions when one views the world as empty. This Viewpoint is concretely illustrated by `Sariputra's` transformation.

The Ch'an School belongs to the tradition of `Tathagatagarbha` thought which advocates the universal enlightenment and the transcendence of differences in the realm of hsiang or external characteristics. No wonder that it is in the Ch'an School that Chinese Buddhist nuns received more recognition and respect than in any other schools. This positive attitude toward women is definitely related to the doctrines on which the Ch'an School is based.

Most of the records of the Ch'an Bhiksuni masters are found in the collections of biographies of the Ch'an masters, such as the Cheng-te ch'uan-teng lu, Hsu-ch'uan-teng lu (the Sequal of the Transmission of Lamp), Wu-teng-huei-yuan (the Collection of the Five Lamps), Wu-teng ch'uan shu (the Complete Collection of the Five Lamps), and many others. There are about three dozen of `bhiksunis` recorded in these historical Ch'an literature. Most of these records, with a few exceptions, are brief. They do not provide much information of life stories about these female Ch'an masters, but they contain their concise Ch'an talk. Of the recorded Ch'an bhiksuni masters, we find only Tsung-chih, Liao-jan, Liao T'ieh-mo, Yuan-chi, Shih-chi and the anonymous nun, who had an encounter with T'an-kung, are prior to the T'ang dynasty.

The others belong to the five post-T'ang sub-sects of the Ch'an School, mostly Lin-chi Sect, of the Ming and Ch'ing dynasties.

In the teaching of the First Patriarch of the Ch'an School one finds the doctrine that laid the foundation of Ch'an's positive attitude toward women. The First Patriarch Bodhidharma's teaching is contained in the Two Entrances and Four Practices, which was recorded by his disciple T'an Lin and cited in the Leng-chia shih-tsu chi (Records of the Masters and Disciples of the Lanka School). According to this text, Bodhidharma taught that although there are many enter the Way, they can be summarized in two categories, namely, the Entrance by Principle and entrance by Practice.

The Entrance by Principle means to realize the Principle through the teaching (chiao), that is, to have a firm belief that all sentient beings possess the same true-nature, which however, is not manifested, because it is obscured by afflictions. If one is able to forsake the false, return to the true, abide in "wall-contemplation", reach a state of equality between oneself and others, the worthies and the worldlings, one is in accord with the Principle.9

The innately pure nature of enlightenment possessed by all sentient beings is the core of Ch'an teaching. It transcends all dualites and distinguishing characteristics (`laksana`), including maleness and femaleness. As the Sung Ch'an master Ta-hui Tsung-kao (1089-1163) said in his instruction to his female disciple Miao-yuan:

> *"Concerning this matter, every one is equal, regardless of being a man or woman, noble. Why? At the assembly for the preaching of the Lotus Sutra, the Buddha simply helps one girl to become a Buddha, and at the assembly for preaching the Nirvana Sutra, he only helps one butcher to become a Buddha."*

Again he said,

> *"Can you say that she is a woman, and women have no share [in enlightenment]? You must believe that this matter has nothing to do with [whether one is] male or*

female, old or young. Ours is an egalitarian Dharma-gate that has only one flavor."

Ch'an masters not only recognized women's spiritual capabilities, but also in some cases were so open-minded that they were willing to request instruction from `bhiksunis` This liberal attitude toward women actually is consistent with Ch'an's anti-authoritorian spirit. The Ch'an literature mentions enlightened women who challenged, confounded and inspired monks to become enlightened. These records not only indicate the women's self-confidence and spiritual achievement, but also shows the liberal and open-minded attitude of the Ch'an School toward women.

The first `bhiksuni` mentioned in the Ch'an literature was Bodhidharma's disciple Tsung-chih. Her life-story is unknown. The Ching-te chuan-teng lu tells us that before returning to India after many years of teaching in China, Bodhidharma asked his disciples to relate their realization of the Dharma.

Tao-fu said, "I perceive that the Buddhist path is transcending language and words and yet not separating from language and words." Bodhidharma said, "You have attained my skin."

The Bhiksuni Tsung-chih said, "What I comprehend is like joyfully seeing the `Aksobya's` Buddha-land." After seeing it once, you never see it again.

"You have attained my flesh," said Bodhidharma. Tao-yu said, "The four elements are originally empty and the five aggregates are non-existent. Not even one thing of what I comprehend is attainable."

"You have attained my bone," said Bodhidharma. Finally Huei-k'e made a bow to the teacher and stood aside in silence.

Bodhidharma said, "You have attained my marrow."

This is the story of how the Dharma was transmitted to the Second Patriarch Huei-k'e. Bhiksuni Tsung-chih was one of Bodhidharma's most advanced students. Although she was not the top disciple, the mere fact that she played a role in the scene of the Dharma-transmission is itself very significant. We might say this makes a good beginning for `bhiksunis` in the Ch'an tradition.

The most well-known female Ch'an master is Mo-shan Liao-jan. Her story is very revealing. Actually she is the only nun who is given a record of her own in the Ching-te ch'uan-teng lu. The story goes like this:

When the monk Kuan-ch'i Chih-hsien14 was travelling from place to place [looking for a teacher] he came to Mo-shan. Before [meeting Liao-jan, the abbess of Mo-shan] he said to himself, "If this place is all right, then I will stay. If not, then I will overturn the Ch'an plaftform (that is, show up the ignorance of the teacher)." So saying, he entered the hall.

Liao-jan sent an attendant nun to ask: "Are you merely sightseeing, or did you come for the Buddha Dharma?"

Chih-hsien replied, "For the Buddha Dharma." Liao-jan then ascended to her seat. Chih-hsien asked for instruction. Liao-jan asked,

> *"Where did you start your journey today?" Chih-hsien replied, "From the entrance to the road (lit., from the mouth of the road)."*

Liao-jan said, " Why didn't you cover it?" Chih-hsien had no reply. He then for the first time performed a kneeling bow to her. He asked,

> *"What is Mo-shan (lit., summit mountain)?" Liao-jan said, "Its peak is not exposed." Chih-hsien said, "What is the occupant of Mo-shan like?" Liao-jan replied, "(S)he has neither male nor female form (hsiang.)" Chih-hsien shouted,*

"Why doesn't she transform herself?" Liao-jan replied, "She is not a spirit, nor a ghost. What would you have her become?"

Chih-hsien at this could only submit. He became a gardener at the nunnery, where he stayed for three years.

Later after Chih-hsien became a Ch'an master, he acknowledged Liao-jan's instruction to his disciples. He said, "When I was at Lin-chi's place I got half a ladle, and when I was at Mo-shan's place I got another half-ladle. Obtaining the full ladle that has enabled me to satisfy my hunger until today."

The encounter of Mo-shan and Chih-hsien is very significant in that firstly, a Ch'an monk was, in his pursuit of enlightenment, was willing to break the tradition against a monk's learning from or bowing to a nun. Secondly, after obtaining enlightening instruction, he publically gave her credit, and lastly, the Ch'an School as a whole was willing to acknowledge the spiritual superiority of the nun by documenting this event.

According to the tradition, the Buddha set eight rules as pre-conditions before he admitted women to the Sangha. These rules put the Bhiksuni Sangha in a subservant position to Bhiksu Sangha. Five of the rules specify that the bhiksunis should get instruction or certification from bhiksus on such matters as the Vassa, Uposatha ceremony, Upasampada initiation and so forth. Nowhere in the Buddhist scriptures does it indicate that a bhiksu should request instruction from a bhiksuni. The monk's bowing to a nun was unacceptable in Buddhist tradition. Thus, what Chih-hsien did represented a radical breaking away from male-dominant mentality.

However, one can still sense the attachment to the hsiang between male and female from the conversation between Liao-jan and Chih-hsien. Liao-jan's anwser of "its peak is not exposed" to Chih-hsien's question of "what is Mo-shan?" implies the invisibility or transcendence of hsiang. Yet Chih-hsien did not get the message. So he asked what the occupant of Mo-shan (lit. summit mountain) was like. In reply Miao-jan spelled out clearly that she (Mo-shan) had neither male nor female form. Still Chih-hsien was not satisfied with the answer and therefore pushed her further by asking her to transform herself. The implication was that to prove her realization, she should transform herself into a male before she could get enlightened as the Dragon Girl did. Liao-jan flatly rejected the idea. It is not known whether she had the supernatural powers to perform a sex transformation. But this is not the point. Her refusal to even accept the idea of the transformation indicates that she had already comprehended the irrelevance of gender to the realization of Buddhahood.

Another significant point that Liao-jan made in the encounter was that she had no interest in supernatural powers, because it had nothing to do with enlightenment. It is true that Buddhism teaches that after a practitioner achieves a certain degree of realization, spiritual power develops. An Arhat is said to possess six supernatural powers (`sadabhijna`):

1. the ability to see anything anywhere,
2. the ability to hear any sound anywhere,
3. the ability to know the things in all other minds,
4. the knowledge of all former existences of self and others,
5. the power to be anywhere or do anything at will, and
6. the supernatural consciousness of the waning of vicious propensities.

Even so, Liao-jan understood that it is through enlightenment that supernatural powers are manifested, rather than that supernatural powers enhance enlightenment. Furthermore, supernatural powers are not attainable exclusively by Buddhists. It is possible for anyone who has deep religious and spiritual cultivation to develop some kind of super-normal powers. In some cases even non-human beings, such as gods, spirits or ghosts, have supernatural powers that ordinary human beings do not have. This is why she insisted that she was neither a spirit nor a ghost.

As mentioned above, the status of women culminates in the triumphant appearance of Srimala in the `Srimala-Sutra` and the Goddess in the `Vimalakir-nirdesa Sutra`. `Srimala`, an advanced female Bodhisattva, not only is the leading character in a Buddhist sutra, but actually teaches the very important doctrine of `Tathagatagarbha` thought, which happens to advocate the existence of universal Buddhahood. The Goddess, a symobolic figure, represents a liberal "feminist" who boldly teaches the doctrine of `sunyata` to `Sariputra`, a representative of the conservative traditon. It emphasizes that all conventional distinctions-maleness versus femaleness, good versus evil, `samsara` versus nirvana and so forth--are simply illusory. Liao-jan, although he lived in a male-dominated Chinese society, had fully comprehended the Buddhist teaching of `sunyata` and the unconventional spirit of Ch'an. She truly demonstrated that she had the same calibre, vision and insight as `Srimala` and the Goddess.

In Ch'an literature, Liao-jan's story was cited often in the Dharma-instruction given by Ch'an masters. For example, Hung-chih mentioned it several times in the Hung-chih Ch'an-shih kuang-lu. Ta-hui and Yuan-wu also recounted her story as examplary when they were giving instruction. This liberal and open-minded attitude is characteristic of Ch'an as is clearly illustrated in Ch'an Master Wu-hsiang's instruction to a woman.

The daughter of an official named Mu-jung was very interested in Buddhist teaching. She came to Wu-hsiang and-said, "As a woman, I am not free in that I have the obstacles and the five hindrances. I am restricted by the female body. Now I come to you for the purpose of cutting off the source of transmigration [in the cycle of life and death]."

Wu-hsiang then said, "Since you have the aspiration [to seek liberation], you are already a great 'man'.....Non-thought is non-male; non-thought is non-female."

As the story indicates, the woman had accepted the traditional image of women and the idea of the inferiority of the female body. To counteract this stereotyped misconception, Wu-hsiang pointed out that as soon as she had brought forth the aspiration for enlightenment, she trancended the gender limitation. The realm of enlightenment, which Wu-hsiang interpreted as non-thought, is neither male nor female.

It is interesting that a story with similar theme is also recorded in the Ching-t'e chuan-ting lu. However, in this case, discrimination against bhiksunis is apparent, at least outwardly. When an anonymous `bhiksuni` wanted to give a formal Ch'an lecture, the monk T'an-kung said to her, " A `bhkiksuni` , as a woman, should not give a Ch'an teaching." The `bhiksuni` said,

> *"What do you have to say about the eight-year-old Dragon Girl becoming a Buddha?"*
>
> *"The Dragon Girl can do eighteen kinds of transformations. Can you just make one transformation for this old monk?"*
>
> *"Even one can transform oneself, one is nothing but a wild-fox spirit.22" said the `bhiksuni` .*

T'an-kung then kicked her out.

From the dialogue we can see that T'an-kung, first of all, challenged the ability and right of the `bhiksuni` to teach. Then when she rebutted that even an eight-year-old girl can realize Buddhahood, T'an-kung brought up the traditional view of sexual transformation, which signifies the identity of maleness with enlightenment. Like Liao-jan, the `bhiksuni` simply denied the validity, relevance and necessity of such transformation. However, the two stories turn out differently. One ends in the monk's paying homage to the nun, while the other ends in the monk's kicking out the nun. When we say that the Ch'an School takes a more liberal and sympathetic attitude toward women, it does not necessarily mean that every Ch'an monk does so.

Another nun who played an important role in the process of a monk's seeking for enlightenment is named Shih-chi. Her biography cannot be found anywhere in the Buddhist literature. However, she is mentioned in the biography of the monk Chu-chih. Chu-chih lived in a hut at Chin-hua Mountain. One day Shih-chi, wearing a bamboo hat and holding a metal staff, showed up in the front of his hut. She circumambulated Chu-chih three times and said to him,

> *"If you can say it, I will take off the hat [to pay homage to you]"*
>
> *She asked three times, but Chu-chih was not able to say anything. As she was leaving, Chu-chih said to her,*
>
> *"It is getting late. Please stay overnight."*
>
> *"If you can say it, I will stay," she said.*

Again, he could not say anything. After the nun left, he said to himself,

> *"Although I have the physical form of a man, I do not have the insight of a man."*

He then decided to leave the hut to look for teachers for instructions. However, that very night a mountain spirit told him that he did not need to go away, for a great monk would come soon. A few days later, a monk named T'ien-lung came to the hut. -Chu-chih greeted him and told him about the encounter with Shih-chi. T'ien-lung said nothing, but pointed with one finger. Seeing this gesture, Chu-chih was immediately enlightened. After that, every time a monk came to him for Dharma instruction, he said and did nothing but point with one finger. His unique instruction was later called "One-finger Ch'an".

As we can see from this story, `Bhiksuni` Shih-chi must have been an enlightened Ch'an practitioner and had enough confidence in herself to challenge a monk. What she pressed Chu-chih to express was his understanding of the essence of Ch'an; in other words, what insight he had attained. After he failed the test, he felt ashamed to have a male's body but not the insight of a male, while Shih-chi, who had a female body, had the insight of a male. His feeling reflects the male's sense of superiority. It was his sense of inferiority in terms of spiritual achievement that urged him to seek enlightenment. In this case, feminist insight plays a very positive and helpful role.

Again, there is an account of a nun named Yuan-chi, recorded in connection with a monk. According to the Fo-tsu-kuang-mu, Yuan-chi lived in Ching-chu Ssu and had practiced meditation in a cave at the T'a-jih Mountain. She and her brother, a monk named Yuan-chueh, had studied with Huei-neng, the Sixth Patriarch of the Ch'an School. She wrote a book called Yuan-ming-ke (the Sound of Perfect Enlightenment), which was said to be comparable in insight to the Cheng-tao-ke (The Sound of Realizing the Way) by the famous monk Yung-chia.

Later, when Yuan-chueh died in Wu-t'ai Mountain, he stood upside down, and nobody was able to overturn his dead body. His sister Yuan-chi went to Wu-t'ai Mountain, scolded the body and knocked it down. This story showed that Yuan-chi had a better understanding of the spirit of Ch'an than her brother.

The Chiao-t'ai pu-teng lu recorded an encounter between Bhiksuni Yuan-chi and the Ch'an master Tsueh-feng Yi-ts'un. It says that Yuan-chi was ordained during the Ching-yun period in the T'ang Dynasty (710-711). After practicing meditation in the T'ai-jih Mountain for some time, she went to see Tsueh-fung. He asked her,

"Where did you come from?"

"The T'ai-jih Shan (the Mountain of Great Sun)," she replied.

"Has the sun risen?"

"When the sun has risen, it will melt Tsueh-fung (literally, the peak of the snow mountain)," she said,

"What is your name?" Tsueh-fung asked.

"Yuan-chi (literally, a good weaver)."

"How much can you weave a day?" Tsueh-feng asked.

"Stark naked," she said

After saying this, Yuan-chi paid her homage and went out. After she had taken a few steps, Tsueh-fung said, "Your robe is dragging on the floor. "Upon hearing this, Yuan-chi turned her head immediately and looked at the hem of her robe. Hsueh-fung burst into laught and said, "How stark naked!" In this story Yuan-chi and Tsueh-fung challenged each other to unveil the subtlety of Ch'an by using double-entendre, one of the typical techniques employed by Ch'an masters to instruct their students and also by the students to indicate their insight. By answering "stark naked", Yuan-chi demonstrated a good grasp of Ch'an's essence. Yet she instinctively turned around to check her robe when Tsueh-feng tricked her by telling her that it was dragging on the floor. This reaction, of course, shows that she was not completely free of attachment. Apparently, Tsueh-feng got the upper-hand in this "match".

Another Ch'an `Bhiksuni` master who had a difficult encounter with a enlightened Ch'an monk is Iron Grindston Liu (Liu T'ieh-mo). The dates of her birth and death are unknown. She lived in a hut ten miles from Kuei Mountain where the famous Ch'an master Kuei-shan Lin-yo (771-853 A.D.) 29 lived. She had practiced Ch'an for a long time and her insight was said to be very deep. One day she went to visit Kuei-shan. The Pi-yen lu records their conversation:

Iron Grindstone Liu arrived at Kuei-shan. (Commentary: Being unaware of the difficulty of getting accommodations, this old lady was out of her depth.)

Kuei-shan said, "Old cow, you've come!" (Comm. Check! A probing pole, a reedshade. Where should you look to see the obscurity?)

The Grindstone said, "Tomorrow there's a great communal feast on (Wu) T'ai Shan; are you going to go, teacher?" (Comm. The arrow is not shot to no purpose. In China they beat the drum, in Korea they dance. The letting go was too fast, the gathering in is too slow.)

Kuei-Shan relaxed his body and lay down. (Comm. The arrow got him. Where will you see Kuei Shan? Who realizes that in the far-off misty waves there is another more excellent realm of thought?) The Grindstone immediately left. (Comm. She's gone. She saw the opportunity and acted.)

What is the meaning of all this? The author of the Pi-yen Lu cited a Ch'an master named Feng-hsueh who commented as follows:

Haven't you heard how a monk asked Feng Hsueh, "When Kuei-shan said, 'Old cow, so you've come' What was his inner meaning?" Feng Hsueh said, "In the depths of the white clouds the golden dragon leaps." The monk asked, "When Iron Grindstone Liu said, 'Tommorrow there's is a great communal feast on T'ai Shan; are you going to go, Teacher?' what was her inner meaning?" Hsueh said, "In the heart of the blue waves the Jade Rabbit bolts."The monk asked, "When Kuei Shan immediately lay down, what was his inner meaning?" Hsueh said, "Old and worn-out, decrepit and lazy, days without concern; lying idly deep in sleep, facing the blue mountains."

`Bhiksuni` Iron Grindstone Liu was described as being like a "stone-struck spark, like a lightening flesh." What she said in the Ch'an conversation must mean something. Kuei Mountain is over six hundred miles from Mt. T'ai; how then did she expect Kuei-shan to go to the feast? The question was nothing but a response to Kuei-shan's statement on her arrival: one "gathering in", one "letting out". Kuei-shan answered her question by doing nothing but lying down. This is another "gathering in" and when she left in silent. this symbolizes "letting out". They "answer back to each other like two mirrors reflecting each other, without any reflection image to be seen."

Iron Grindstone Liu had another encoutner with yet another Ch'an teacher named Tsu-hu.

Tsu-hu said, "Are you Iron Grindstone Liu?"

She answered, "Yes."

Tsu-hu said, "Turn right and turn left."

She said, "Venerable, don't be upside down (meaning unreasonable)."

Tsu-hu then struck her.

An encounter between the great master Chao-cho and an anonymous nun is recorded in the Wu-teng hui-yuan. One day the nun asked Chao-cho, "What is the meaning of the secret meaning?" Chao-cho made a gesture of pulling out something. The nun said, "Your Venerable still has this." Chao-cho said, "It is you who still have this."

The secret meaning here refers to the ultimate truth, which according to Buddhist teaching transcends words. This is why Chao-cho used a gesture, instead of words, to express the inexpressible truth. However, the nun disagreed that Chao-cho still needed a gesture to point out the ultimate truth, for the use of an action to indicate truth is unnecessary and, in fact, an attachment. Chao-cho refuted her by saying that her attachment to the notion of unattachment is an even greater attachment.

As we can see from the above disscussion, the tension between sexual discrimination and Buddhist ideals of egalitarianism exists throughout Buddhist literature, including the Chinese Ch'an tradition. Comparatively speaking, the Ch'an School espouses the most sympathetic and liberal attitude toward women. In a tradition full of misogynist prejudice, as found in Chinese society, it is very significant that Chinese Buddhist women not only found their places on the path leading to religious fulfillment and self-realization, but also have played an active and instructive role in helping their male counterparts to achieve their religious goal. When one's genuine spiritual achievement, rather than human gender and social status, is taken as the sole criterion, human civilization makes a great step forward. For making this contribution, the Ch'an School deserves recognition.

9

Reflections of the Feminine in Japanese Buddhism

INTRODUCTION

Buddhism teaches a way of life that leads to universal Enlightenment without regard for sex or even species. The idea that women might not be able to gain Enlightenment has been entertained, but by a minority; likewise, despite the fact that rebirth in the human realm is considered to be the most propitious, it has not been considered impossible that spiritual practice could be pursued while in non-human form. Indeed, many Jataka tales describe the spiritual practice undertaken by the Buddha and some of his senior disciples when reborn in the animal realm. However, within the human realm, not all have been considered to be born equal and different schools of Buddhism, to varying degrees, have made broad claims about the spiritual capacities of men as group and women as a group, women being understood to be at a disadvantage in relation to men. Japanese Buddhism, in particular, has been characterised by a persistent anti-feminism, with women being portrayed as not simply disadvantaged but positively dangerous.

This article will briefly look at several key Japanese Buddhist texts and representations formulated by men about women and question whether there is anything characteristically 'Buddhist' about them at all. I shall argue that rather than offering privileged insight into the special difficulties faced by women practitioners, these texts are in fact about men and their troubled relationship with women.

As Bernard Faure points out, in Buddhist texts generally:

> *Woman is conspicuously absent, or she appears in as much as she is an element of the Buddhist discourse on sexuality: not for herself, as individual, but as one pole of attraction or repulsion in a gendered male discourse about sex. Denied the role of a subject in this discourse, she is primarily the emblem of larger generative, karmic or social processes, with positive or negative soteriological value (1998:14).*

My reading of Buddhist texts 'about women' is influenced by feminist theorists such as Laura Mulvey who, like Faure above, argues that in all man-made representations, women are a 'silent image' which she describes as 'bearer of meaning, not maker of meaning' (1975:7). As I will show below, the meanings that have been projected on to women in Japanese Buddhism have been largely negative.

A MIRROR FOR WOMEN?

The title of this article is taken from a popular medieval religious tract written in 1300 by Muju Ichien, a Rinzai Zen monk. The title is derived from a passage in the text where Muju encourages his female readers to 'make these precepts her constant companion [as she would a mirror]' and thereby establish herself as 'a person of sensibility, a follower of the Way'. Despite the fact that the readership of the text is envisaged as female, the advice offered by Muju is remarkably non sex-specific; indeed it is standard Buddhist ethical teaching, liberally sprinkled with citations and examples from Canonical scriptures.

It is not until near the end of the text that Muju directly addresses women when he states that 'Many serious instances of the sins of women, among the unregenerate who are all deluded, are cited in the sacred scriptures and commentaries.' Referring to a list drawn up by the seventh-century Chinese monk Dosen, he outlines the 'Seven grave vices of women'. These are:

(1) they arouse desire in men;

(2) they are jealous;

(3) they lack empathy;

(4) they are only concerned with their appearance;

(5) they are deceitful; and

(6) they are without shame.

The first six in the list are hardly surprising and, indeed, could have been listed in the same order in a Christian tract of the same era. What is most interesting about this list is the seventh 'sin' of women:

> Seventhly, their bodies are forever unclean, with frequent menstrual discharges. Seeing that both pregnancy and childbirth are both foul and the afterbirth unclean, the evil demons vie for possession while the good deities depart (cited in Morrell 1980:68).

While the first six sins of women are character traits that some women might be expected to embody more than others, just as some men might, the last sin is a physiological condition which affects all women equally. It is only the seventh sin that can be characterised as specifically female.

The notion of women's inherently defiled and defiling nature derives from Muju's literalistic understanding of karma. Earlier in the text he explains that stingy and greedy people are born into poverty, that the haughty are born into low castes, and that those who violate the precepts are reborn with defective sense organs. Although Muju does not make the connection in the text, he believed that beings were not born as women by chance but that rebirth in such a defiled body was the result of some negative past-life action.

Muju accepted the belief, prevalent in popular Buddhism of the time that women were by nature unclean. This understanding has significant implications for women's spiritual practice because of the great emphasis placed upon ritual purity in Japanese religion, both Buddhist and Shinto. Since women were at all times unclean, it was not possible for them to enter the holiest parts of monastery or temple compounds, or in extreme cases, to even set foot on the mountains where these retreats were built . More importantly, according the Menstruation Sutra (Ketsubon kyo), which was widely read in Japan from the time of Muju until the end of the nineteenth century , every time a woman bled, she polluted the ground and the waters that were used to make offerings to the Buddhas and severely offended them. As a result she was constantly accruing negative karma, the result of which was rebirth in the 'Bloodpond Hell'.

This is a startling claim and is clearly in conflict with fundamental Mahayana principles such as emptiness and non-duality. How can a woman's body be 'inherently' defiling? This paradox was addressed by certain male exegetes of this sutra such as the author of the early nineteenth-century work, 'Random Stories about the Buddhist Ceremonies - The Origin and Transmission of the Ketsubon kyo' , who reasoned that:

Because they were born as women, their aspirations to Buddhahood are weak, and their jealousy and evil character are strong. These sins compounded become menstrual blood, which flows in two streams each month, polluting not only the earth god but all the other deities as well (cited in Takemi 1983:235).

In this analysis of women's 'sins', their lack of spiritual aspiration, jealousy and evil nature are the volitional characteristics that result in negative karmic effects or sa.mskaaras. Women's menstrual blood is here not seen so much as a symbol of these negative volitions but a physical effect of them just as obesity might be the result of greed. Despite the fact that this position can be undermined using basic Mahaayaana principles, it does not seem to have been criticised by Buddhist teachers in any systematic way. Indeed, the 'defilement' of women became the paradigmatic Japanese Buddhist view.

Women in Japanese Buddhism were defined by their bodies in a way not paralleled by representations of men. Indeed, women as a class became identified with the flesh and with carnality in a manner strikingly similar to Christianity which suggests that this representation of women is not characteristically 'Buddhist' but rather 'male' . Faure points out how the Buddhist male establishment was 'unable or unwilling to distinguish between biological constraints and the arbitrary constraints imposed by society' (2003: 105). In Buddhist thought, there really is only one gender - femaleness - since maleness is not considered problematic and not subject to interrogation. While we have a multitude of examples of male clerics discoursing on the disadvantages of female rebirth, there is no balancing voice that comes from women themselves where maleness is held up to scrutiny or regarded as problematic or 'other'. Men are viewed within Buddhism as somehow less gendered than women, already, by virtue of their male anatomy, closer to an ideal of androgyny.

A further way in which women tended to be reduced to the purely physical occurs in a variety of Japanese Buddhist images of female cadavers. These images, designed for contemplative meditation, occur throughout poetry, narrative literature, woodblock prints and paintings from the thirteenth to the nineteenth centuries and are not paralleled by similar depictions of male cadavers (Chin 1998: 277). This is not a characteristically Japanese practice but, as the work of Liz Wilson (1995, 1996) has shown, is paralleled by the treatment of the female corpse in Pali and Sanskrit literature.

As Wilson argues, the use of the female (never the male) corpse as an image for contemplation means that, paradoxically, women become the teachers of men, but it is not what is going on in women's minds which is important, it is the physical process of decay taking place in their bodies. She comments that through horrific transformation, the woman's body is 'made into a display board for the Dharma' (1995:95). Women, as symbols of 'the material,' are once more understood to be tied up with the physical body in a way not paralleled by representations of men.

WOMEN'S 'FIVE OBSTRUCTIONS'

Closely connected with the Japanese Buddhist idea that women were somehow defiled is the doctrine of the Five Obstructions (or 'Hindrances'). According to this teaching, women are excluded from five forms of rebirth, namely rebirth as a Brahma god, the god Sakra, the tempter Maara, a Wheel-turning king or a Buddha. The idea behind this doctrine is that there is something inherent in the state of 'woman' that means she cannot, while in female guise, attain the very highest or most powerful forms of existence as symbolised by the list of the five great beings. Similar to the defilement arising from menstruation, the 'five obstructions' are understood to be internal to the state of 'woman,' something that women have brought upon themselves through previous negative actions.

Faure sees the origin of this list as a 'technical or juridical restriction' arising from the rules subordinating women to men within the sangha, but points out-how within Japanese Buddhism they came to be interpreted as a 'moral and ontological inferiority' deriving from women's impurity - since rebirth as a woman was not a morally neutral state but resulted from bad karma (2003:63). These two teachings regarding women occur throughout Japanese Buddhist texts of all periods and can be said to characterise the Japanese Buddhist view of women, at least until recent times.

How did Buddhist women position themselves in relation to this male-centred view which scripted them as objects in a discourse which characterised them as defiled, defiling and by their very nature incapable of attaining the highest and most powerful forms of rebirth solely on the basis of their female body? It is difficult to answer this question because it is hard to find examples from the Japanese tradition where women speak about themselves in their own voice.

However, there is an interesting incident in Murasaki Shikibu's eleventh-century novel The Tale of Genji that suggests that women may not have always taken these teachings too seriously. Murasaki was a woman of high birth serving as a lady-in-waiting to the Empress who, more than any other figure in Japanese literary history helped define Japanese prose literature. Denied her own teacher, Murasaki was a child prodigy who had learned the Chinese classics by listening outside the door to the lessons provided for her less able brother. Her father is reported to have said that he wished she had been born a boy for then she would have been able to rise to a position in the world that best suited her remarkable abilities. Murasaki, as a capable, highly intelligent, well-educated woman might be expected to have shown a certain disdain towards male-dominated narratives positioning women as inherently defiled and inferior, and in one passage in her novel in particular, this would seem to be the case.

The passage occurs late in the novel, after the death of the hero Prince Genji and concerns the speculations of Genji's son, Prince Kaouru, about the nature of women. Kaouru's thoughts, upon overhearing his mother's religious practice, are narrated thus:

His mother was at her devotions, morning and night, but he thought it unlikely that the efforts of a weak and vacillating woman could transform the dew upon the lotus into the bright jewel of the law. A woman labours under the five hindrances, after all. He wanted somehow to help her towards a new start in another life.

Above is the translation offered by Edward Seidensticker and it would seem to rehearse the usual definitions of women as weak, lacking consistency and in need of help and advice from men (even their sons!) in order for them to make any spiritual progress. Most invidious of all is the notion that a woman's primary efforts should be directed towards rebirth as a man (as is suggested by the phrase 'a new start in another life').

However, as Edward Kamens (1993: 389) points out, the phrase translated 'the five hindrances' is not the usual itsutsu no sawari, but the circumlocution itsutsu no nanigashi which might more properly be rendered as 'the five something-or-others' or 'the five whatsits'. Murasaki's audience would have had no trouble identifying the 'five something-or-others' as the 'five obstructions' and would certainly have been able to list them, so why did Murasaki choose this circumlocution?

One possible interpretation would be that she was indicating a certain disdain for this particular 'teaching,' or expressing an ironic attitude towards the idea that women are 'hindered' by what she lightly refers to as 'the five whatsits'. As Kamens points out 'dismissal, condescension, and exclusion - of women, by men - are what the itsutsu no sawari topos is all about' (1993:393).

Could Murasaki, a brilliant and unusually well-educated woman, here be expressing disdain for the tradition which regarded her as inherently defiled and handicapped by her female birth? After all, Kaouru is Murasaki's creation, the condescending attitude he expresses towards his mother is scripted by Murasaki herself. Anyone who reads the entire novel could not miss the irony of this passage in which Kaouru, at best a confused and melancholy adolescent, thinks how he might best 'help' his mother on her spiritual path. In this passage, is Murasaki not subtly undermining the condescending attitudes held towards women by many of the male nobles at Court who were far less able than herself?

JAPANESE FEMINIST CRITIQUES OF BUDDHISM

Japanese feminists have criticised the various negative Buddhist representations of the female form in much the same way as western feminists have attacked Christianity. Hitomi Tonomura asks 'What does it mean to illuminate the Buddha's truth [of impermanence] consistently through the female body? Does it not configure the female as an object of observation, an entity disassociated from her own humanity?' (cited in Chin 1998:278). And it is worth raising the question, although it is impossible to answer in the context of the present article, what was the effect upon women believers who, less self-confident than Murasaki, were expected to see themselves 'mirrored' in these representations?

Japanese feminist criticism of Buddhism has been harsh and thoroughgoing and certain Buddhist teachings have been interpreted as underlying mainstream views of women that assign them to a lesser place in Japanese society even today. Minamoto Junko, for instance, has written a number of books in Japanese criticising the patronising tone of many popular Buddhist tracts written by male monastics for their female lay followers. These texts were often gathered together in compilations such as the sixteenth-century Collection of Teachings for Women (Nyonin kyoke shu). Many of the passages in this collection, which was used for purposes of proselytization by the Pure Land School, rehearse the negative views about women that had by this time become widespread. These include the notion that women have been abandoned by the Buddhas because of their sinful nature, and that they cannot generate the bodhicitta or become a Buddha while in a woman's body. The reasons given are again connected to women's essential nature:

> This is because women are possessed of a feckless and grasping nature, and their actions are day and night motivated by thoughts of attachment and a jealous heart. Caring only for themselves, they heap envious calumny upon the heads of others and generate the karma of evil and impropriety (cited in Minamoto 1993:97).

These attitudes were very pervasive and were still characteristic of Japanese Buddhism in the nineteenth century as the abbot of the Honganji order, Honnyo (1778-1826) illustrates in a letter to female disciples:

> Women are said to be afflicted with the Five Obstacles and the Three Subjugations (i.e. they must obey their fathers in childhood, their husbands in marriage, and their sons in widowhood). Because they are terribly sinful, they are abandoned by the buddhas of the ten directions and fall into the hells with no hope of salvation' (cited in Minamoto 1993:92).

The above text shows a fusion of Buddhist and Confucian (the Three Subjugations) beliefs which, from our modern understanding of Buddhism, expresses an extreme wrong view: that women as women are unable to make spiritual progress (i.e. are 'beyond hope of salvation').

Unfortunately, Minamoto reads the negativity expressed towards women in Japanese Buddhist texts as a fundamental characteristic of Buddhist teaching that goes back to the Buddha himself (she notes the Buddha's seeming reluctance to admit women to the sangha) and she fails to draw attention towards those few teachers within the Japanese Buddhist tradition (of whom Dogen is the most remarkable) who showed great impatience with male disciples' attitudes towards women.

Nor does she discuss Mahaayaana texts and bodhisattvas that stress women's spiritual potential, as if in response to the popular view of them as inferior and defiled. These other Buddhist voices, stressing that 'femaleness' has no bearing on an individual's ultimate spiritual capacities, and identifying obsession with gender difference as a spiritual hindrance in itself, should not be underestimated when giving an account of the Buddhist attitude towards women.

However, given the great volume of calumny directed towards women by men recorded in the Japanese Buddhist tradition, it is no surprise that, within the Japanese context, Minamoto concludes, 'Buddhism has operated as a philosophy that blocks modernization' (1993:113). She regards Buddhism as a hindrance to the development of women's rights in Japan, identifying Buddhism as 'a reactionary philosophy' chained to outmoded and discredited views of 'women' (1993:113).

It is perhaps no surprise that it has not been the traditional Buddhist sects that have attracted large numbers of women practitioners in recent times, but the syncretistic 'new religions' that have become identified with women spiritual leaders in Japan.

CONCLUSION

The above texts and representations of women taken from the Japanese Buddhist tradition say nothing about the actual nature of women; indeed, in a Mahaayaana context, it would be doctrinally impossible to elucidate just what this 'real' nature might consist of. Instead, these texts express the ambivalent and, at times, hostile attitudes held towards women as a group by men as a group.

Throughout the representations discussed above, 'femaleness' seems to function as a repressed dark side and 'woman' as a repository into which men empty themselves of negative traits which could be said to characterise men as much as they do women. In so doing, the male figure becomes the norm, the archetypal 'human' figure, the ideal Buddhist practitioner, and the proto-Buddha-to-be. Women, to the extent that they are acknowledged at all, are men's shadows, lesser beings who are presented more as spiritual hindrances to men than as spiritual practitioners in their own right.

In a seminal essay, feminist anthropologist Sherry Ortner asks the question 'Is female to male as nature is to culture?', an apt question in relation to a recent book attempting to explain the Buddhist view of women . In the course of her research, Ortner was struck by how 'in every known culture, women are considered in some degree inferior to men' (1974:69). Rejecting an explanation based on biological determinism (that women somehow 'lack' a potential inherent in the male body), Ortner instead suggests that women have repeatedly been identified with the world of 'nature' whereas men have been associated with the world of 'culture'.

As she argues, women are 'seen as representing a lower order of being, as being less transcendental of nature than men are' (1974:73). This is certainly true of the Japanese

Buddhist tradition where women's menstruation became a particular site of morbid fascination for male monastics, leading to the development of an entire 'sutra' dedicated to the topic.

That such a belief could come to dominate the Japanese Buddhist tradition is curious in the light of the strong Mahayana influence in Japan and the antinomian tendencies displayed by characteristically Japanese schools such as Zen, Nichiren and Pure Land. Why were key Mahayana teachings such as the emptiness of all phenomena and the non-duality of nirvana and samsara not used to question the curious insistence that women were 'by nature' both defiled and defiling?

There is nothing 'Buddhist' about the negative view of women expressed in much of the Japanese Buddhist tradition; in fact, these views show startling similarities to those elucidated at great length by another elite group of male monastics in the Christian tradition. In Christianity, too, 'women' became the bearer of the 'nature' archetype, associated with sensuality, carnality and death.

Given the radical nature of the Mahaayaana dialectic which insists upon a fierce interrogation of the dualistic structures which determine our conceptualisation of the world, it is odd that such obviously mistaken views about the nature of women came to be widely held throughout Japanese Buddhism.

The texts described above are, therefore, a mirror for men in that they show how dangerous it can be when a single group within society controls not only who can speak, but also what is said. As Sherry Ortner has argued: 'Ultimately, both men and women can and must be equally involved in projects of creativity and transcendence. Only then will women be seen as aligned with culture, in culture's ongoing dialectic with nature' (174:87).

Throughout most of Japan's history, women were denied access to the social institutions that would have enabled them-to participate along with men in the project of cultural production. When some outstanding women such as Murasaki, quite by accident, managed to access the education reserved for men, they showed themselves to be more than capable of equalling and even surpassing the achievements of men. Murasaki Shikibu stands out in the Japanese tradition as a clear example that the 'Five Whatsits,' despite male monastics' claims to the contrary, may not have been such a hindrance to women after all.

Bibliography

Basham, A. L.: *History and Doctrines of the Ajivikas,* London, Luzac, 1951.

Bell, Sir Charles: *Portrait of a Dalai Lama: The Life and Times of the Great Thirteenth,* Boston, Wisdom Publications, 1987.

Bloom, Alfred: *Shinran's Gospel of Pure Grace,* Tucson, University of Arizong Press, 1965.

Collins, Steven: *Nirvana and Other Buddhist Felicities: Utopias of the Pali Imaginaire,* Cambridge, Cambridge University Press, 1998.

Cook, Elizabeth: *Holy Places of the Buddha,* Berkeley, Dharma Publishing, 1994.

Cowell, E. B.: *Jataka Stories,* London, Pali Text Society, 1956.

Dargyay, Eva M.: *The Rise of Esoteric Buddhism in Tibet,* Delhi, Motilal Banarsidass, 1977.

Dayal, Har: *The Bodhisattva Doctrine in Buddhist Sanskrit Literature,* London, Kegan Paul, 1932.

Dresser, Marianne: *Buddhist Women on the Edge: Contemporary Perspectives from the Western Frontier,* Berkeley, North Atlantic Books, 1996.

Eppsteiner, Fred: *The Path of Compassion: Writings on Socially Engaged Buddhism,* Berkeley, Parallax Press, 1988.

Gombrich, Richard F.: *Buddhist Precept and Practice,* Delhi, Motilal Banarsidass, 1991.

Gonda, Jan: *Vedic Literature: Samhitas and Brahmanas,* Wiesbaden, 1975.

Hakeda, Yoshito S.: *Kukai, Major Works,* New York, Columbia University Press, 1972.

Haldar, J. R.: *Early Buddhist Mythology,* New Delhi, Manohar, 1977.

Horner, I. B.: *Women Under Primitive Buddhism,* Delhi, Motilal Banarsidass, 1975.

Johansson, Rune E. A.: *The Psychology of Nirvana,* New York, Doubleday, 1970.

Keown, Damien: *The Nature of Buddhist Ethics,* New York, St. Martin's Press, 1992.

Lamotte, Etienne: *The Suramgamasamadhi Sutra,* London, Curzon, 1998.

Mookerjee, Satkari: *Buddhist Philosophy of Universal Flux,* Delhi, Motilal Banarsidass, 1980.

Morrell, Robert: *Early Kamakura Buddhism: A Minority Report,* Berkeley, Asian Humanities Press, 1987.

Nyanatiloka, A.: *Guide through the Abhidhamma Pitaka,* Kandy, Buddhist Publication Society, 1971.

Poppe, Nicholas: *The Twelve Deeds of Buddha,* Seattle, University of Washington Press, 1967.

Powers, John: *Wisdom of Buddha: The Samdhinirmocana Sutra,* Berkeley, Dharma Publishing, 1994.

Sarkisyanz, E.: *Buddhist Backgrounds of the Burmese Revolution,* The Hague, Martinus Nijhoff, 1965.

Seneviratne, H. L.: *Rituals of the Kandyan State,* Cambridge, Cambridge University Press, 1978.

Shaw, Miranda: *Passionate Enlightenment: Women in Tantric Buddhism,* Princeton, Princeton University Press, 1994.

Sprung, Mervyn: *The Problem of Two Truths in Buddhism and Vedanta,* Boston, Reidel, 1973.

Strong, John: *The Legend of King Asoka,* Princeton, Princeton University Press, 1983.

Taylor, J. L.: *Forest Monks and the Nation-state,* Singapore: Institute for Southeast Asian Studies, 1993.

Thomas, E. J.: *The Life of the Buddha as Legend and History,* London, Routledge & Kegan Paul, 1927.

Wells, Kenneth E.: *Thai Buddhism, Its Rites and Activities,* Bangkok, Christian Bookstore, 1960.

Williams, Paul: *The Reflexive Nature of Awareness,* London, Curzon, 1997.

Index

C

D

□□□